PERSPECTIVES ON THE AGRO-EXPORT ECONOMY IN CENTRAL AMERICA

Perspectives on the Agro-Export Economy in Central America

Edited by

Wim Pelupessy
Lecturer in Development Economics
Tilburg University, The Netherlands

University of Pittsburgh Press

Published in the USA by the University of Pittsburgh Press, Pittsburgh, Pa. 15260

Published in Great Britain by Macmillan Academic and Professional Ltd

Printed in Hong Kong

Library of Congress Cataloging-in-Publication Data

Perspectives on the agro-export economy in Central America / edited by
    Wim Pelupessy.
        p.   cm. —(Pitt Latin American series)
    Includes bibliographical references and index.
    ISBN 0–8229–1164–7
    1. Produce trade—Central America.   2. Exports—Central America.
    3. Agriculture—Economic aspects—Central America.   I. Pelupessy,
    Wim.   II. Series.
    HD9014.C462P47   1991
    382'.41'09728—dc20   91–2232
                                                                   CIP

To Elisabeth, compañera de vida

Contents

List of Tables

List of Figures

Preface

For a long time a small number of export crops has formed the backbone of economic activity in Central America. There are few real alternatives to this traditional orientation towards agrarian exports, in spite of a regional based industrialisation and the expansion of tertiary sectors since the 1960s.

After a period of continued overall economic growth in the years 1960–75, all countries in the region suffered from an economic crisis of considerable dimensions, with strongly reduced growth rates of Gross Domestic Product. Falling international prices and smaller quantities sold on world markets, social unrest and in some cases armed conflicts, and poor economic policies, have all increased enormously the deficits on balance of payments and government accounts and accelerated the rates of inflation, capital flight and unemployment. Foreign borrowing has not provided solutions but only increased the external indebtedness of the countries. Therefore in most cases programmes for structural adjustment to increase the supply of exportables, as proposed by international financial institutions, have been put forward. However, postwar strategies depending on exports have not brought much improvement in the employment and income situation of the majority of the population and the conditions of absolute poverty have not decreased during the last decades. For a viable recovery strategy an evaluation of present and future functioning of the traditional agro-export sectors is needed.

This book was developed out of a seminar for researchers on this topic from several European countries and Central America, which was organised in December 1987 by the Development Research Institute of Tilburg University in the Netherlands. In the introductory chapter the main findings of the book are reviewed in the context of the actual economic debate on Central America. The next chapter gives an overview of the historical development of the agrarian export sectors, while the later chapters present results of up-to-date research on the international commodity markets and fieldwork on the organisation of production within the region, but mainly in the war-torn countries of Nicaragua and El Salvador. Hopefully these results can serve as building blocks for the empirical foundations required in the design of a reconstruction strategy to support the on-going process of negotiations for peace and justice in the region.

I wish to thank Jenny Pearce for revising the text and translating Chapter 1 (by Edelberto Torres-Rivas) from Spanish, and Frans Thielen for giving assistance in the preparation of the typescript.

WIM PELUPESSY

List of Abbreviations

ACP	African, Caribbean and Pacific countries who signed the Lomé Treaty with the European Community
AID	Agency for International Development (USAID)
APP	Area of People's Property
ATC	Association of Rural Workers
BANAMERICA	Nicaraguan Bank of America Conglomeration
BANIC	Bank of Nicaragua Conglomeration
BCR	Central Bank of Reserve
BFA	Agrarian Development Bank
CAS	Sandinista Agricultural Co-operative
CCS	Credit and Services Co-operatives
CEDLA	Centre for Study and Documentation on Latin America
CEPAL	Economic Commission for Latin America and the Caribbean (English: ECLA or ECLAC)
CIERA	Agrarian Reform Research Centre
CONAL	National Cotton Commission
COPAL	Salvadorean Cotton Co-operative
CRIES	Regional Coordinator of Social and Economic Research
CSUCA	University Council of Central America
CUDI	University Centre for Documentation and Information
DEA	Department of Agricultural Economics
EC	European Community
ECLA	Economic Commission for Latin America (Spanish: CEPAL)
ECLAC	Economic Commission for Latin America and the Caribbean (Spanish: CEPAL)
EDUCA	Central American University Editorial
ENAL	Nicaraguan Cotton Enterprise
ENIA	National Enterprise for Agrarian Inputs
FAO	Food and Agricultural Organization
FINATA	National Land Financing Agency

FLACSO	Latin American Faculty of Social Sciences
FMLN	Salvadorean Liberation Front
FUSADES	Salvadorean Foundation for Economic and Social Development
GATT	General Agreement on Tariffs and Trade
GSP	General System of Preferences
IBRD	International Bank for Reconstruction and Development
ICADIS	Central American Institute for Documentation and Social Investigation
ICO	International Coffee Organisation
IDB	Interamerican Development Bank
IICA	Interamerican Institute for Co-operation in Agriculture
INCAFE	National Institute of Coffee
INIES	Institute of Social and Economic Research
ISIC	Salvadorean Institute for Coffee Investigation
ISTA	Salvadorean Institute for Agrarian Transformation
IVO	Development Research Institute
MAG	Ministry of Agriculture and Cattleholding
MIDINRA	Ministry of Agricultural Development and Agrarian Reform
OEDEC	Executive Office of Inquiries and Census
OIT	International Labour Organization (ILO)
PROAGRO	Nicaraguan Enterprise for Agricultural Products
SIECA	Secretariat for Central American Economic Integration
SPP	Secretariat of Planning and the Budget
STABEX	Stabilisation Fund for Exports
TNC	Transnational companies
UNAG	National Union of Farmers and Cattlemen
UNAN	National Autonomous University of Nicaragua
UNCTAD	United Nations Conference on Trade and Development
USAID	*See* AID

Notes on the Contributors

Harrie Clemens is Research Associate in the Department of Agrarian Economy of the Free University of Amsterdam, Amsterdam, the Netherlands

E. V. K. FitzGerald is Professor of Development Economics at the Institute of Social Studies (ISS), The Hague, Netherlands

Jan P. de Groot is Lecturer in Development Economics in the Economics Faculty of the Free University of Amsterdam, Amsterdam, the Netherlands

Elmar Meister is Research Associate at the University of Marburg, Marburg, West Germany

Massimo Micarelli is Member of the Institute for Relations between Italy and the Countries of Africa, Latin America and the Middle East (IPALMO), Rome, Italy

Wim Pelupessy is Lecturer in Development Economics in the Faculty of Economic Sciences of Tilburg University, Tilburg, the Netherlands

Frans Thielen is Research Associate at the Development Research Institute (IVO) of Tilburg University, Tilburg, the Netherlands

Edelberto Torres-Rivas is General Secretary of the Latin American Faculty of Social Sciences (FLACSO), San Jose, Costa Rica

Introduction: The Central American Agro-Export Economy – Issues and Debates

E. V. K. FitzGerald

Since colonial times – and possibly before – Central America has been geared to the primary-export economy. Primary commodity exports still represent one half of material production and two-thirds of foreign exchange earnings, and are thus the single most important growth factor in the region. Although this sector embraces mining, forestry and fishing it is dominated by agricultural exports organised mainly in large enterprises which obtain labour and food from the mass of small peasant farmers who surround them. Despite the large profits to be made and high production growth rates in the three postwar decades, sustained economic development has not been attained in Central America. On the one hand, the cyclical transformations of demand patterns in metropolitan markets have led to the familiar cycles of 'boom and bust' over the centuries. Industrialisation – other than export processing – has been a recent phenomenon in Central America, with serious shortcomings in terms of efficiency and market size. On the other hand, the emergence of a social structure made up of repressive regimes, footloose foreign investors and an impoverished semi-proletarian peasantry, has led to a weak civil society subject to both US intervention in support of its oligarchies and mass movements against exogenously induced modernisation.

In late 1987 a seminar was held at Tilburg by the Development Research Institute (IVO) to evaluate the functioning of and changes in the traditional agro-export sectors in Central America. Researchers from The Netherlands, Germany, Italy and Britain met with Central American colleagues to present the results of fieldwork within the region and case studies of international market conditions. The present volume is based on the papers presented at the seminar.

1

It is fitting that the first chapter in this volume is by Edelberto Torres-Rivas of the FLACSO, undisputed *doyen* of Central American social scientists. It is a very good example of what has become the generally accepted interpretation of the historical political economy of the region. Torres-Rivas argues that Central America was inserted into the world commodity market and local social structures were subordinated thereto; indeed he goes as far as to argue that agricultural exporting was the means by which the metropolitan powers imposed order upon the periphery. He traces the effects of agro-exports on the concentration of property ownership and the way that specific products have involved determinate enterprise forms under peripheral capitalism – such as haciendas for coffee, plantations for bananas and peasant plots for foodgrains. Torres-Rivas concludes that popular mobilisation against this local model of capital accumulation has coincided with depressed world commodity markets to generate the present crisis. He draws the logical conclusion from this argument – that the agro-export model, at least in its traditional form, offers no future because it cannot address the strategic issues of growth (that is, industrialisation) and equity (that is, basic needs entitlements), but can only exacerbate them.

The external vulnerability and internal underdevelopment of Central America are not really in debate between economists. The question is rather one of the relationship between these characteristics and the scope for an alternative more viable development model. The official interpretation of the Central American institutions themselves tends to be 'structuralist' but is none the less inspired by the accepted historical discourse (ECLAC, 1984). The United Nations Commission for Latin America and the Caribbean stresses the inequitable nature of world commodity markets and the difficulty of access for new producers; so that the lack of external resources has constrained incipient industrialisation. The ECLAC also holds that concentrated income distribution has prevented the emergence of a broad internal market, while low rates of investment out of available savings have reduced growth and basic needs satisfaction.

In one of the most impressive of recent historical studies of agro-exports in the region, Williams (1986) shows how the postwar introduction of modern agribusiness from the USA in response to changes in export demand necessarily involved repressive labour control, expropriation of peasant land and ecological destruction in order to remain profitable. The export boom of the 1950s and 1960s introduced new staples – particularly cotton and beef – which raised growth rates and reduced the region's traditional reliance on coffee and bananas. The agribusiness model – generously financed by the IBRD, IDB and USAID – stimulated exports and profits but also generated the landlessness and repressive regimes which made these societies so vulnerable to the world system shocks of the 1970s, and led inexorably to political collapse in the 1980s. Here again the implication is that a more viable economic development model combining growth with equity would require a shift away from agro-exports, and most probably towards self-sufficient economies.

On the basis of these and other studies, a certain 'conventional wisdom' has emerged to the effect that agro-exports are intrinsically inimical to development in Central America. In other words, it is the activity as such – as opposed to the social organisation of production and exchange involved, or the distribution of the surplus generated – that is the problem. In the 1980s this is often contrasted with the desirable aspects of peasant-based food agriculture in terms of employment generation, national self-reliance, steady growth and democratic potential (Barraclough and Marchetti, 1985). This contrasts sharply with the preferred alternative model of the 1960s – import-substituting industrialisation – upon which the Central American Common Market had itself been founded. The dilemma is that despite the evident failure of export-led growth to provide adequate food production and distribution for the population in the past, to strengthen basic needs provision requires foreign exchange which can only be realistically obtained by modernising the export sector and restructuring domestic manufacturing to support domestic agriculture (FitzGerald, 1985). The problem, then, is of designing a food-constrained accumulation strategy where industrialisation does not take place at the expense of the peasantry, which means that the role of agro-exports must be defined *as part of the concept of food security itself*.

There are, as might be expected, significant differences of opinion as to the scope for such redefinition of the agro-export model. Bulmer-Thomas (1987), for instance, traces structural changes in the sector over the last century and stresses both the ability of local élites to negotiate with international markets and the real progress towards industrialisation since the Second World War – itself financed by agro-exports. Despite a common pattern of extreme social inequality, he argues that wide differences do exist between the five republics and their respective regimes. This implies that there is scope for social reform and industrialisation within the existing framework. In contrast, Weeks (1985) argues from a Marxist perspective that the chief problem of Central America is the incomplete transition from a feudal to a capitalist social formation, from which arises the continued need to repress agro-export labour in order to sustain profitability. According to this interpretation, national development can only be achieved by revolutionary change – even to establish an indigenous capitalist class, let alone socialism. None the less, despite their evident theoretical differences both authors see the continuation of the outward-orientated growth model as the only foreseeable scenario. For Bulmer-Thomas a possible solution is to be found in non-traditional agro-exports (that is, in new staples according to the product cycle model): while for Weeks the prospect is of continued stagnation until the social system is transformed under the pressure of its contradictions.

Scholarly enquiry has only recently begun to contribute to the policy debate directly, above all in relation to the discussions about a 'regional economic alternative' that have accompanied the political negotiations within the Contadora and Esquipulas frameworks. Irvin and Gorostiaga (1985) report on one of the first such conferences, held at The Hague in 1983, which stressed the need for the expansion of regional industry linked to basic needs provision and financed by the better use of agro-export possibilities for Central America in the medium term. This latter point was derived from the consensus of agreement that neither regional autarchy nor a rapid shift towards industrial exports are realistic possibilities for the immediate future. It has since been argued that if industrialisation was only possible in the past due to the surplus generated by agro-exports (Irvin, 1988), it is equally clear that *new* staples would be required in order to break into new markets (Zuvekas, 1989). In analytical terms it can be shown (FitzGerald, 1985) that agro-exports are potentially equivalent to a 'capital goods sector' for small economies in that the size of net foreign exchange earnings determines the availability of producer goods.

The most recent policy research on the possibility of reviving the Central American Common Market reported in Irvin and Holland (1989) and Conroy (1989) underlines this point. Two key conditions for industrial reconstruction and food security *on a regional basis* are: (a) the refunding of intra-regional trade through debt relief and the reconstruction of financial institutions; and (b) the expansion of extra-regional exports to at least double their present level. The former would be based on food and light manufacturing, and could lead in the longer run to manufactured exports to world markets. However, successful rehabilitation of industry and economic infrastructure will depend upon the latter increase in agro-export income to fund it directly or to service the consequent debt.

Such a combination is a central element in the 'Special Plan of Economic Co-operation for Central America' adopted last year by the United Nations General Assembly (UN, 1988), which in turn forms the basis for support by the EEC (1988). The UN plan is the first truly international initiative for regional reconstruction, and proposes a multilateral programme of some US $4 billions in aid. Its two main pillars are (a) the renewal of regional economic integration, and (b) improved institutional mechanisms for trade with the rest of the world. Considerable spare capacity in regional industry is identified, which can quickly be rehabilitated with adequate working capital. More than any other factor the loss in traditional export earnings during this decade is held to lie at the root of the regional crisis. Thus the UN logically emphasises both intra-regional trade revival *and* export diversification while correctly placing priority on easing the foreign exchange constraint on imports, a goal most effectively accomplished by addressing the issue of debt directly (Caballeros, 1987; FitzGerald and Croes, 1989).

Unfortunately, although the new US administration appears to have abandoned the prospect of direct military intervention in the region, there is every indication that the Kissinger Plan (1984) is still regarded as official policy – a decision which will presumably also condition the actions of the multilateral funding agencies towards Central America. Clearly, the return to the old agro-export model implied by the Kissinger formula (which is based on increased sugar and beef quotas, low-wage manufactured exports, foreign investment incentives and 'security' aid) will exacerbate rather than resolve the crisis, if experience is any guide.

What is required, therefore, is greater understanding of the way in which the agro-export sector itself functions. Two points in particular require elucidation:

(a) the nature of the marketing channels for agro-export products, and in particular the distribution of profits between producers and merchants on the one hand and access to new markets on the other;

(b) the impact of agro-export production on the local economy, and in particular the potential of alternative enterprise and property forms to improve the linkage effects.

The papers in this collection do in fact contribute substantially to our knowledge on these two topics. This is not the place to summarise them in detail – a duty that is ably done by the editor in Chapter 7 – but rather to draw out their contribution to the broader economic debate outlined above.

In Chapter 2 Micarelli examines EEC markets for coffee, cotton and banana in detail, examining the effect of oligopsony, government regulation and competitive sourcing in depressing commodity prices and thereby Central American export income. He reveals a complex power structure which none the less can – as in the case of coffee – provide opportunities for greater market penetration, particularly if alliances with wholesalers can be established. The results may not merit great optimism but do justify a greater effort to diversify and develop the agro-export sector itself. In Chapter 3 Meister takes up the role of coffee in more detail for the case of West Germany, giving fascinating details of market and cost structures. What this reveals is that Central America receives little more than a third of the final price as export income, and that production costs represent as little as one-tenth of what the consumer pays. These data would seem to indicate that much more could be gained by negotiating along the marketing chain than by reducing local production costs – especially wages.

The fieldwork on agro-export production conditions reported in Chapters 4, 5 and 6 show that production conditions and forms of enterprise organisation in agro-exports can (and do) vary quite widely between the five Republics and over time, according to the pattern of property relations and government policies. In Chapter 4, de Groot and Clemens show how the supply of cheap labour essential to the profitability of traditional Nicaraguan coffee producers was undermined by the Sandinista land reform, which gave peasant families other opportunities for more remunerative use of their family labour power. However, they argue that experience since 1979 has shown that other forms of labour mobilisation (such as students), the retention of labour on large farms through family plots or co-operatives, and technological change could reduce the need for such large amounts of seasonal wage labour. In other words, distributive land reform can be compatible with agro-exports.

In Chapter 5 Thielen compares cotton production in El Salvador and Nicaragua, where access to land and systems of marketing have differed between the two countries in recent decades. The quite distinct agrarian reforms applied in the 1980s – involving not only land tenure but also state intervention in marketing and finance – have created alternative accumulation models of both capitalist and socialist content. In Chapter 6 Pelupessy compares coffee and cotton in El Salvador, showing that middle-farmers have survived the crisis rather better than large ones. He argues that although the boom period for these products is clearly finished, there do exist alternative forms of social organisation – particularly co-operatives – that could combine economic viability with social equity.

If an agro-export sector can be established that generates the required amount of foreign exchange and involves acceptable forms of ownership, then the remaining issue is whether profitable production of tropical staples necessarily requires a cheap labour force, particularly for harvesting. To the extent that in the long run world prices for primary commodities are determined by low labour costs in *other* Third World producers (for example, coffee in Kenya) using a common technology, then Central America must necessarily maintain a comparably low wage rate in order to compete. Of course the region enjoys a certain 'rent' due to its superior soil quality and proximity to major markets, but the problem is crucial to the wider distributive effects of agro-exports.

This topic is not addressed directly in this volume, although it is implicit in the discussion of the endemic labour supply problem. Historically (Torres-Rivas) the peasants had to be driven from the land in order to create a 'reserve army' of labour and keep wages down. Distributive land reform (de Groot and Clemens) reverses this mechanism: a solution is posed in terms of fusing ownership with family labour supply or by organising production in smaller family enterprises (Pelupessy). However, this does not resolve the problem of seasonal labour, while the higher implicit wage of a co-operative member may reduce long-run accumulation potential. The greater profitability of small farms may well arise from more intensive work, or the employment of 'surplus' women and children. Alternatively, low (that is, internationally competitive) wages can be made acceptable to the labour force by providing cheap food and free social services. Traditionally the former has been achieved by distorting the internal terms of trade and impoverishing the food-producing peasantry. The latter may require taxation of other sectors of the economy or generate inflation.

Of course, as Lewis (1969) pointed out, it is the general inefficiency of tropical food production per head that brings about the internationally low wages in the first place, because the subsistence sectors of tropical economies offer an even lower return on labour. Given that the return on capital is not determined by productivity in the crop itself but rather by the general rate of profit on capital, however productive the world sugar (or cotton or coffee) industry may become, the benefit mostly accrues to metropolitan purchasers in the form of low prices.

How then to combine efficiency with welfare? The secret seems to lie in the success stories of small exporting ventures as far apart as Taiwan and Scandinavia. Increased efficiency in food production and public investment priorities in rural health and education raise real living standards without raising wages. The unit cost of labour can decline (and allow wages to rise without reducing profitability) without reliance on capital-intensive technology if work intensity rises with income incentives and the workforce is more highly skilled. The added advantage is that such a workforce is more flexible in terms of both adapting to new production techniques and products, and even in relocation if basic needs become citizen entitlements. A protected (that is, non-traded) wage-goods and social services sector thus becomes essential for export efficiency and not an alternative. In the case of Central America, this can be attained by distributive land reform and community-based organisation of primary health, education and housing.

This does not mean that the possibilities of economic growth in Central America are anything other than modest without massive injections of external reconstruction assistance and renovation of the production structure. Nor does it imply that the profound social transformation necessary to overcome poverty would be easy, even were it to be supported by the donor community. It is essential to recognise, however, that there does exist space for manoeuvre and progress *within* the agro-export model once political changes are under way. At the time of writing (early 1989) there is still a real opportunity for peace in Central America, underwritten by the Esquipulas Accord between the five Presidents and strongly supported by the European Community.

This Accord explicitly recognises the need for a new economic development model in order to secure social justice; and was subsequently specified in joint proposals made by the five governments to potential aid donors (SIECA, 1988). The position of the Bush

Administration is still ambiguous at best. However, most authoritative sectors of US opinion from across the political spectrum such as Fagen (1987), Feinberg and Bagley (1986) and Best (1987) agree that the long-term national security interests of the USA would best be served by a stable and non-aligned Central America. This would require explicit recognition of the need for fundamental socio-economic reforms in order to guarantee minimal living standards and civil rights for the poorer half of the regional population. With this position the European governments seem to concur.

The detailed studies of the agro-export sector contained in this collection are so timely because sound empirical foundations are essential to the design of feasible development strategy; particularly in the areas of commodity market analysis and that of the organisation of production itself. Without such a strategy, political progress will come to a halt and the hopes of the poor and the powerless be betrayed once again. Clearly more policy research needs to be done *within* the region itself, as the bibliography to this paper indicates: but a decade of conflict has left the relevant institutions in ruins.

The role that the IVO has played in stimulating the debate between European and Central American scholars reflected in this volume is all the more significant for the record of Tilburg University – along with other Dutch institutions of higher education – in helping to rebuild the shattered intellectual infrastructure of Central America. The transfer of research skills, knowledge of metropolitan export markets and analysis of Third World experience could well become a rare example of the benign application of the Ricardian principle of comparative advantage.

Bibliography

Barraclough, S. and Marchetti, P. (1985), 'Agrarian Transformation and Food Security in the Caribbean Basin', in Irvin and Gorostiaga (eds), op. cit.
Best, E. (1987), *US Policy and Regional Security in Central America* (London: Gower).
Bulmer-Thomas, V. (1987), *The Political Economy of Central America since 1920* (Cambridge: Cambridge University Press).
Caballeros, R. (1987), 'External Debt in Central America', *CEPAL Review*, no. 32, pp. 123–48.
Conroy, M. (ed.) (1989), *Transformation or Continuing Crisis? The Future of the Central American Economy* (Austin, Tx: Texas University Press).
ECLAC (1984), 'The Crisis in Central America: Origins, Scope and Conse-

quences', *CEPAL Review*, no. 22, pp. 53–80.

ECLAC (1986), 'Central America: Bases for a Reactivation and Development Policy', *CEPAL Review*, no. 28, pp. 11–48.

EEC (1988), 'Joint Economic Communiqué of the Hamburg Ministerial Conference on Political Dialogue and Economic Co-operation between the European Community and Its Member States, and the Countries of Central America and the Contadora Group (29 Feb.–1 March)' (Brussels: Commission of the European Community/DGI).

Fagen, R. (1987), *Forging Peace: The Challenge of Central America* (New York: Blackwell).

Feinberg, R. E. and Bagley, B. M. (1986), *Development Postponed: The Political Economy of Central America in the 1980s* (Boulder, Col.: Westview).

FitzGerald, E. (1985), 'Planned Accumulation and Income Distribution in the Small Peripheral Economy', in Irvin and Gorostiaga (eds), op. cit.

FitzGerald, E. (1989), 'The Economic Crisis in Central America: an European View', in Conroy (ed.), op. cit.

FitzGerald, E. and Croes, E. (1989), 'The Regional Monetary System and Economic Recovery', in Irvin and Holland (eds), op. cit.

Irvin, G. (1988), 'ECLAC and the Political Economy of the Central American Common Market', *Latin American Research Review*, vol. 23 (3) pp. 7–29.

Irvin, G. and Gorostiaga, X. (eds) (1985), *Towards an Alternative for Central America and the Caribbean* (London: Allen and Unwin).

Irvin, G. and Holland, S. (eds) (1989), *Central America: The Future of Economic Integration* (Boulder, Col.: Westview).

Kissinger, H. (1984), *Report of the President's Bipartisan Commission on Central America* (New York: Macmillan).

Lewis, W. A. (1969), *Aspects of Tropical Trade, 1883–1965* (Stockholm: Wicksell Lectures).

SIECA (1988), *Reunión de Vice-presidentes: Plan de Accion Inmediata* (Guatemala: Secretaria Permanente del Tratado General de Integracion Economica Centroamericana).

UN (1988), 'Special Plan of Economic Co-operation for Central America', *42nd Session of the UN General Assembly* (A/42/949) (New York: United Nations).

Weeks, J. (1985), *The Economies of Central America* (New York: Holmes and Meier).

Williams, R. (1986), *Export Agriculture and the Crisis in Central America* (Chapel Hill, N.C.: University of North Carolina Press).

Zuvekas, C. (1989), 'Central America's Foreign Trade and Balance of Payments: the Outlook for 1988–2000', in Conroy (ed.), op. cit.

1 Perspectives of Central America's Agro-Exporting Economy

Edelberto Torres-Rivas

1. BRIEF RETROSPECTIVE INTRODUCTION

There are numerous examples of how exports have been a dynamic and essential factor in the growth of national economies. This has undoubtedly been the case in the past; external trade was the best indication of the general health, not just economic health, of any society. The Central American experience is an outstanding example of how articulation with the world market in the second half of the nineteenth century conditioned the formation of the nation state, with all that this means as a totality of causes and effects. In fact, the region could only survive the post-independence period (1821) through the export of certain primary products. But these were short cycles and insufficient to reorder the colonial legacy. It was also evident that the incorporation of these societies into the flow of international trade could only be carried out through *agricultural products* when 'comparative advantage' worked effectively.

The export of primary products was important in a multiplicity of ways, as much for the purchasing economies like England (initially), Germany and the United States (later), as for the sellers. To the latter it was of essential importance, and helped reorganise the old social, cultural and political order. It meant finding an adequate solution to the problem of commercialising local agriculture. All this was not exactly a 'model of development' imposed from outside, as it is usually described today. Export agriculture was a *mode of implanting and ordering capitalism* in the periphery. Social classes were reproduced and modified on the basis of this form of reproduction and accumulation of capital, together with forms of political and cultural life, until appropriate conditions for and limits to the development of the nation state were established.

11

Central America has not been homogenous even in its colonial origins. Incorporation into the world market is an eloquent example of the deep differences which have laid down the pattern of development of each of the societies in the region. With the assumption that national differences and differences in the form of reproduction were important, it is possible to establish a structural model of agro-exporting activity divided into three periods or stages. These reflect the forms adopted by the social organisation of labour, the resulting agrarian structure, the labour market which accompanied that organisation of production, technical advances and the importance of capital and foreign interests, including not only investment capital but also the nature of intermediary commercial capital. The three periods do not follow chronologically.

In the first period coffee was the export product *per se*, which began to be marketed abroad at the beginning of the sixth decade of the nineteenth century in Costa Rica and successively in Guatemala, El Salvador and later Nicaragua. Honduras only became a coffee exporter in this century. The cycle of coffee continues almost up to the third period. The organisation of coffee production, in its strictly agricultural aspects, called upon political factors which, based on the cultural traditions and on the prevailing population profile, produced the basic structure of agricultural production: *the great coffee estate* (sometimes only partially utilised large farms or *latifundia*) which forced into being the *colono* (farm labourer tied to the estate), the migrant labourer and the sharecropper; *the medium rural property*, which capitalised slowly but looked towards the market making use of all family labour; and the *subsistence peasant economy*, which does not make use of all family labour and whose access to land has diminished gradually but not disappeared, forced to combine ever more intense incursions into the labour market and/or the sale of a part of the harvest destined for family consumption.

The great coffee estate appears typically in Guatemala and El Salvador; the medium-sized rural property more in Costa Rica but also in Nicaragua. And the small subsistence plot or *minifundio* appears in all the countries alongside the large-scale properties, but with significant variations which cannot be gone into in this chapter. Here, we only point to typical situations. From a theoretical point of view, as Baumeister suggests (1987:2,3) it is important to point out that coffee is only produced in the peripheral countries and destined for the developed markets of Europe and the US. Only national owners figure in the formation of the costs of production and their control. Foreign capital is present as credit and commercial capital and in almost all the countries is important in the agro-industrial stage (control of the coffee-husking plants), sharing profits with the nationals and acting as oligopolistic purchasers. This is mostly the case in Guatemala, less so in Costa Rica and Nicaragua, and even less in El Salvador.

In the second period bananas emerge, produced on the capitalist plantation. It is a modernised form of agriculture, based on the transfer of capital, technology and managerial practices from abroad. The plantation is always North American and forms an 'enclave economy', because of its relative isolation from the local market and its vertical links (of all the stages of production) with the metropolitan economy. It appears first in Costa Rica at the end of 1880, it develops fully in Honduras and finally in Guatemala. The enclave plantation reinforces other points made by Baumeister; the central countries participate fully as productive capital, without sharing with the nationals the surplus value extracted from a rural wage-labour force, which soon becomes the most important nucleus of workers in the region. Obviously, the plantation was formed through concessions from the state, with political protection. It was set up alongside the large coffee estates, not competing with it in the land or labour markets, and sending all its production abroad.

These are the origins of the most outstanding feature of Central American agriculture. The medium and small properties directed their production of basic grains towards the local or regional markets within each national society, lacking capital and technology, although there were some variants. In Costa Rica, they were more orientated from the beginning toward coffee growing which meant that the supply of labour in the labour market was always poor. In Honduras extensive ranching developed, as well as a numerous and disarticulated peasant economy; in Nicaragua there were no great banana plantations nor extensive coffee estates. The evolution of the wage-labour force was less compulsive in Nicaragua than in El Salvador, completely free in Costa Rica, and difficult and delayed in Guatemala. The *decomposition* (transformation) of the *colono* and the sharecropper as primitive forms of labour were prolonged well into the twentieth century. In the socio-political sphere also, different dominant groups were formed. These élites corresponded to different forms of organisation of coffee production and of other exports, which in their turn had to do with the ownership of land, the social form of production, recruitment of labour, the process of preparing

Table 1.1:   Central America: origin and destination of agricultural production by subsectors in the postwar period (1945–8)   (percentages)

| Origin | Destination | | | Total | Products |
	External market	Own con-sumption	Internal market		
Plantation	25.0			25.0	Bananas, abaca, African palm
Peasant economies	0.2	17.5	7.2	24.9	Maize, beans, sorghum, wheat, vegetables, fruit, sugar
Internal commercial agriculture	5.0	2.5	17.5	25.0	Coffee, cattle, sugar, rice, tobacco, cocoa
Traditional hacienda	20.0	0.0	5.1	25.1	Coffee, wood, cattle
Total	**50.2**	**20.0**	**29.8**	**100.0**	

SOURCE: Torres-Rivas, Edelberto, *Centroamerica: Algunos Rasgos de la Sociedad de Postguerra* (Kellog Institute, 1984) Working Paper no. 25, mimeo.

the bean and finally its export. The class base of the coffee élite, and then that of other products, also shaped the nature of the opposition from the lower classes and the terms and forms of their conflicts (Paige, 1987: 143).

The functional structure whereby *wage-goods* for the internal market were produced on the *minifundia* and export products on the large estates persists, with some important modifications, to this day. But in the third period, which begins after the Second World War, there are important changes in the agrarian profile which do not originate so much in the modernisation of the coffee and banana production structure, but in the introduction of new products such as cotton, beef-cattle, sugar and other products (see Table 1.1).

The agro-exporting economy is reinforced, as a result, under the impulse of international demand, acting again as the dynamic factor which creates or recreates the agrarian structure and society. The most important of such products was without doubt cotton, for the significance which it gained in Guatemala, El Salvador and especially in Nicaragua. There it led to a rapid, painful and late agrarian restructuring, and became after 1955 the axis of the most important reproduction and accumulation in the course of a generation.

The export of beef-cattle in Costa Rica, Honduras, Nicaragua and Guatemala was also important; and sugar in Guatemala, El Salvador, Nicaragua and Costa Rica. A global analysis shows that agricultural exports provide 80 per cent of Central America's foreign exchange.

Table 1.2:   Central America: relative participation of some basic products in the volume of international trade in goods

	1950	*1960*	*1970*	*1977*
Coffee	9.4	9.8	10.1	14.4
Cotton	0.1	1.9	4.2	7.0
Banana	34.8	33.0	32.1	32.1
Sugar	0.1	0.4	1.5	2.6

SOURCE: ECLA, based on official figures.

2. THE MODERNISATION OF THE EXPORTING SOCIETY

Agricultural diversification contributed to the increase in volume and value of regional exports after the war, avoided the negative effects of cyclical fluctuations in the price of individual products and helped modernise production. It also directly favoured the incipient process of industrialisation by contributing the increasing foreign exchange for the import of capital goods, intermediate products and other inputs.

Between 1950 and 1977, agricultural exports increased by twelve times (see Table 1.2), partly due to the fact that the volume of three of the products grew at a higher rate than world demand, revealing the growing regional participation in satisfying that demand (CEPAL, 1986:38). It should be emphasised that during this period the value of exports responded to a greater volume of production rather than a simple rise in prices, the former achieved by acceptable output on productivity levels reached, and the second, by simple conditions imposed by the market. Between 1960 and 1978 the agricultural exports of Central America increased at a real rate of 4.7 per cent, higher than that achieved by any Latin American country in the same period (CEPAL, 1986:96).

The technical modernisation of agricultural production was the result of renovation or readjustment by élites, in particular those who controlled all the productive capital or who had access to banking and commercial capital but were not necessarily landowners; this was the case with cotton. From the point of view of their access to the international market, these products competed directly with similar production in the developed countries. Once again the international price was set from outside, but unlike coffee, the development of the productive forces of developed capitalism influenced the price as much as the fertility of the soil and the cost of labour in dependent capitalism.

The cotton 'boom' is associated with the crisis of the Suez canal and the policy of stockpiling by the large world producers, with the US at their head. The demand for sugar is tied to the redistribution of the Cuban quota by the US in 1961. Finally, the rise of ranching came to depend on a type of beef, low in price and quality, destined for the proliferating 'fast food' chains of North America. In sum, the new 'victory' of agro-exports is associated with geopolitical and economic factors which tie us even more to the US, increasing the external openness and the vulnerability of the region. As a register of its generic importance, Central America had become by mid-1975, at the dawn of the crisis, the most important exporter of cotton and bananas and the second of meat in the total exports of Latin America (41 per cent, 58 per cent and 30 per cent respectively).

This renewal of exports from the countryside also produced a partial redefinition of the sector as a whole: changes in land owner-ship, in the labour market, in social relations as a result of the two previous changes, and of course, in the role played by the State, financial and commercial capital. In the end, Central America's agro-exporting society came to maintain its role in the world market, redefining the dependent character of its economy through diversifi-cation. It is, without doubt, a question of relative modernisation, particularly important in some aspects and with unforeseen but real results in the fields of politics, social and power struggles. We can briefly examine these diverse aspects in order then to look at the agrarian crisis of the 1980s and its prospects.

The first and second periods of this account resulted in an agrarian structure dominated by large-scale ownership and the rural/ commercial bourgeoisie (included here are the banana plantations), together with an extensive peasantry, which slowly shifted from subsistence farming and forced labour to seasonal and incomplete insertion in the market economy. On the one hand, there was the supply of foods for popular consumption and, on the other, seasonal wage-labour, permanent employment and semi-urban or urban mi-gration. Agricultural GDP grew at an average rate which was double the growth of the rural population. Nevertheless, the majority of the peasants grew poorer due to a two-fold situation: the unequal distri-bution of land and the apportioning of the factors of production (such as technology, capital and managerial capacity, all directly associated with external demand) in favour of the large-scale owners. Modernity suppressed the peasantry but did not destroy it.

But while the production of cotton, sugar cane and cattle for export increased the capacity of these modern enterprises to absorb the labour force, it did so at a rhythm below the increase in population. In the case of the first two products, there was a high degree of mechanisation and full freedom to improve technical coefficients, limiting demand for labour.

The agro-export 'boom' of the postwar years had social consequences. For instance, in coffee the coffee estate was renovated with the introduction of the *caturra* variety substituting the *maragogipe*. It did not have to be cultivated in the shade, increased the number of plants per square metre and thus productivity per hectare, and facilitated harvesting. This change converted numerous medium producers into 'agro-exporters', particularly in Nicaragua and Costa Rica, but El Salvador kept its leadership in volume of production and the renovation of the coffee-husking plants. The *colono* or peon tied for life to the estate, disappeared to be replaced by the seasonal agricultural labourer, producing seasonal unemployment for a significant mass of peasant families. This change was most notable in Guatemala and Honduras.

In the case of bananas, the modifications were even more significant. The tropical plantation, studied by Wolf, Mintz, Garcia and so on, which was the form in which European capital penetrated the Caribbean (on the basis of slave labour to produce sugar), began to undergo change in 1950. But the true technical revolution got under way in the 1960s with the substitution of the 'Gros Michel' variety of banana by different forms of 'Cavendish', which were more resistant to Sigatoka disease. The density of planting increased about 30 per cent which facilitated drainage, and field packing was introduced which changed the technical organisation of the export process. This was because it led to the industry's own form of so-called 'manufacturing co-operation', a system of packaging in cardboard boxes which 'industrialised' the final stage, associated today with the use of transatlantic containers.

The shift from the monopsonic-enclave to the international monopoly-enterprise also changed the division of labour. Local producers reappeared to take responsibility for 40 per cent of exports, on average, over recent years. These producers are necessarily tied to the marketing conditions imposed by the 'big three': United Brands,

Castle & Cooke and del Monte,[1] who fix prices, volume, quality and time-schedules. The production and export of bananas today has nothing to do with the tradition of the foreign plantation, nor with the early manifestations of social discontent and the great banana strikes. Nor has it anything to do with the era of the 'banana republics'.

The economic and social scenery changed even more with the new exports. With cotton (Nicaragua, Guatemala, El Salvador, in order of appearance and productive importance) the humid Pacific coast was, literally, occupied by the cotton enterprises. In Nicaragua, it led to the forced displacement of thousands of peasants. They became semi-proletarians, seasonal agricultural labourers in the interior when they were expelled from Chinandega and Leon. In Guatemala, there was no fund of land available from expropriations; instead, former extensive ranching lands or estates formerly sharecropped or worked by *colonos* were 'rearranged'. El Salvador probably had the most tragic experience, because of the violence involved. Lands planted with basic grains were substituted with cotton, rendering the last fertile zone of the agricultural frontier of that country unusable today.

The growth of cotton was important in the 1960s and part of the 1970s, at an average of 13.9 per cent a year regionally. In 1979, the year before the crisis, there were more than 16,750 producers who planted about 400,000 hectares, providing work for 150,000 workers at harvest-time; it was the time of the 327,000 metric tonnes of exports worth more than US $420 million (see Tables 1.3 and 1.4). The price of this growth was not improvement in the prevailing conditions for the rural population nor more agricultural work from a new source of wage labour. It meant the occupation of the last good lands, the expropriation of hundreds of thousands of peasants combined with unresolvable problems of access to land for those previously granted it under various forms of sharecropping and tenancy agreements (*medianeria*). Large-scale ownership became even more concentrated. Wage work increased, but the peasantry was impoverished and a class of large cotton barons emerged closely associated with commercial import/export capital.

The differences between the three cotton countries are important. In Guatemala there is a very high concentration of production in large estates, but with some land rented; in Nicaragua, there are small, medium and large cotton producers, as with other crops, with 60 per cent of the land rented; in El Salvador the monopoly on planting is shared between large and medium-sized estates, but monopolic control centres on the final agro-industrial process, where there were only *three large cotton gins* at the time of the 'boom'. It is worth mentioning that Central America had the highest per unit output of cotton in the world (Sieca, 1966:5) and that the fibre was very highly regarded because it was (or is) cut by hand, keeping it in optimal condition.

As has already been said, the other great export product was beef-cattle, whose origins lay in a coincidence of various factors. Demand from the North American market for meat for popular consumption was the most definitive of these. Sanitary problems and prices in the traditional supplier countries shifted demand. The substitution of native cattle in Central America for the always deficient production of meat and milk began in the mid-1950s, when the first packing plant was installed in Nicaragua, followed by Guatemala, Costa Rica and Honduras.

The role of the state, as with cotton, was decisive in promoting the new export. It acted as an intermediary for public loans from the Interamerican Development Bank, the World Bank and others, facilitated the import of sophisticated packing machinery, linked areas of difficult access with new roads and authorised the greatest destruction of woods (in a decade) for more than a century. Within five years, Central America became an important exporter and at the beginning of the 1960s had over four million head of cattle, which produced 30 million pounds of exports a year. Ten years later, in 1973 there were 22 packing plants which exported 180 million pounds, and over eight million head of cattle. After 1978, at the beginnings of the crisis, there were over ten million head of improved stock which sold 250 million pounds to the North American market, becoming its third supplier of meat. Between 1960 and 1978 the percentage of North American imports of Central American meat rose from five to fifteen per cent (Williams, 1986).

The important work of Robert G. Williams shows what was needed to produce this astonishing result in such a short time. On the demand side there was an insatiable appetite for cheap meat for the huge popular 'fast-food' chains; and on the supply side, the advantages of cattle fed on good pasture, of acceptable quality and at a highly profitable cost. Central American meat, considered locally of excellent quality, was only used to satisfy the poor taste for hamburgers. The link between supply and demand was the revolution in refrigerated transport and the role of the packing plants which served as filter and quality control of the meat produced by national ranchers. The image of the municipal 'abbatoir', where several animals were slaughtered each day, gave way to modern plants, with factory work-methods, which could process up to 500 head of cattle a day.

As with cotton, the ranching enterprise has been a factor in the expulsion of peasant economies in Choluteca (Honduras) and Guanacaste (Costa Rica), and in the extensive region of Matagalpa and the region west of the Gran Lago (Nicaragua) and part of the Pacific, but especially in the region opened up by the building of the Northern Transversal Highway (in Guatemala). The expropriation of former landholdings had devastating social effects from the human point of view; but the deforestation of wooded zones was the greatest disaster the region had known. Land hunger caused by the cattle 'boom' has not been sufficiently recognised nor analysed. The expansive and extensive character of ranching absorbed in a thousand different ways pasture land and natural woods, forest reserves and other types of land. In eight years (1961–9) ranching grew from an area of 3.4 million hectares to over eight million.

The agrarian structure was changed as a result of this frenzy to export meat, resulting in modern but extensive ranching estates. They appear in the census with an average size between 250 and 400 hectares, far from the brutal concentration of land when coffee was established. The concentration of pastureland was less important than the monopolic centralisation of the large packing plants, linked directly to export, where North American capital dominates. In 1979, 28 packing houses were able to process and export US $250 million-worth of meat, almost all for the North American market. The small and medium-size owner could not integrate themselves into the world market. Immediately a divison of roles emerged, between the owners of medium-size ranches, forced to bear the risks of droughts and cattle diseases and epidemics and the need to sell the beef at fixed prices abroad, and the cattle fatteners and large ranchers.

It should be borne in mind that in the case of meat the North American market has been an especially protected one, functioning on the basis of a quota system and strict sanitary controls. The dependency created with this production was even greater than that with coffee, and the vertical structure of the enterprise is reminiscent at times of what exists today between local banana producers and the large transnational companies.

The social effects are not only associated with the accelerated 'decomposition' of the peasant economy, but also with the fact that this is the production which requires least labour. The statistics on this are incomplete, but it is known from a comparative relationship by volume of production that cotton offers six times more work than ranching, sugar seven times, banana nine and coffee thirteen times more.

A brief reference to the last of the three new export products in the postwar period: sugar. This was the least important in relative terms in most of the countries of the region, except El Salvador and Guatemala. The rise of sugar, the introduction of more productive varieties, the renovation or installing of new sugar mills and the expansion of land dedicated to it was also due to North American demand after 1960, with the setting up of national quotas to substitute for Cuban sugar. The production and export of sugar reached significant quantities, but especially at times of high international prices. In fact, Central American sugar was not competitive in those markets and its decline, in many respects, came before the generalised impact of the crisis.

Nevertheless, the crisis in the sugar economy of Central America was not only due to the product's lack of competitiveness in terms of international prices, but because of the application of a restrictive quota policy in the North American market. In 1981, for example, sugar was 5.7 per cent of the total value of the region's exports, whereas in 1985 it was only 2.7 per cent. The estimated losses due to the cutting of the quota for the North American market were calculated at US $23.2 million (1984–5) and US $46.7 million in 1985–6 (Gallardo and Lopez, 1986:92).

3.   THE HURRICANE OF CRISIS STRIKES

The problems of Central America did not in fact begin in 1979. There were many critical moments for the different export products, but the rise of one compensated for the fall of another. The nature of the crisis which began in 1979 was that it affected the entire structure of agricultural exports and all the countries of the region at the same time and in the same way. It raised the possibility that this was not just a conjunctural situation, one moment more in the repeated depressive cycles which affected the coffee republic from the very beginning, but that it may correspond to a more permanent situation and, as a result, to modifications in the structural patterns which shape Central American societies over the long term.

The crisis originated in the strong fall in exports under the dual effect of international prices and the reduction of export volumes. The vulnerability of these societies, open and sensitive to international demand, transmits the crisis of the developed countries with multiplier effects to the heart of the local economy. Between 1979 and 1985 Central America lost 40 per cent in 1970 dollars of what its productive effort would normally have expected (US $1,413.0 million to US $848.0 million; see Table 1.4).

The contraction of the export sector affects the whole of society in many ways which cannot all be dealt with here, and are aggravated by the effects, serious in themselves, of the violent political struggles in three of the countries under analysis. It is clear that national differences are insufficient to explain the homogeneity of the negative effects. Only the political will of the State stands out in some cases more than others, aware of but unable to resolve the dramatic, human effects that stagnation has produced. The most traditional products, coffee and bananas, keep their place in production and volume of exports, but are subject to oscillations in international prices with no possibility of control. On the other hand, the other three products – meat and cotton more than sugar – which had foretold the hoped-for modernisation of the countryside and had certainly meant substantial changes in the export structure, entered into evident decline: production, price, sales volume and so on (see Tables 1.3 and 1.4, and Figures 1.1 and 1.2).

The oscillations in the coffee market correspond to an historic and well-known trend: a drastic tendency to extend a quotas policy and a trend in the opposite direction to 'free' prices in a market oversupplied for certain periods. Nevertheless, it is the only export which in general maintains its price level (except the 1989–90 period) and which still largely contributes the highest amount of foreign exchange in the declining balance of payments. Bananas have also followed a path of late recovery within an oligopolic structure which it has been convenient to maintain in order to sustain prices. Its participation has not diminished in relative terms and perhaps, most important from the point of view of the analysis, is rooted in the internal changes in the relationship of production and marketing, which redistributes profit in favour of the large international companies at the cost of national producers.

But the crisis of agro-exports is part of the North American crisis and has particularly affected the products associated with the postwar

Table 1.3:   Central America: agricultural exports, 1977–85 ('000 metric tonnes)

	1977	1978	1979	1980	1981	1982	1983	1984	1985
Meat	99.60	120.30	121.10	88.40	82.60	72.00	59.60	41.80	49.40
Bananas	2177.00	2237.70	2463.30	2610.30	2268.70	2442.20	2098.00	2241.60	2077.50
Sugar	625.50	458.20	521.00	482.60	459.90	330.50	630.60	450.50	302.30
Coffee	420.20	392.30	547.10	384.00	373.60	332.90	476.60	519.80	565.20
Cotton	298.30	357.90	327.00	219.40	190.20	162.90	158.10	145.50	127.60
Total traditional products	**3620.60**	**3566.40**	**3979.50**	**3784.70**	**3375.00**	**3340.50**	**3422.90**	**3399.20**	**3122.00**
Cocoa	10.00	9.20	7.40	3.80	2.80	2.90	3.00	4.10	3.70
Tobacco	10.70	12.20	12.80	12.70	12.70	12.90	12.90	12.90	12.90
Wood	417.70	337.60	256.30	176.80	201.90	217.10	170.80	149.20	141.40
Plants, seeds, flowers, etc.	4.10	2.40	4.60	7.70	5.40	3.30	4.80	9.10	8.00
Total non-traditional products	**442.50**	**361.40**	**281.10**	**201.00**	**222.80**	**236.20**	**191.50**	**175.30**	**166.00**
Agricultural products	4063.10	3927.80	4260.60	3985.70	3597.80	3576.70	3614.40	3874.50	3288.00
Total exports	**6221.30**	**6010.60**	**6306.30**	**6037.70**	**6003.80**	**5667.00**	**5738.40**	**5547.60**	**5473.60**

SOURCE: Calculations based on SIECA, 'Series Estadísticas Seleccionadas de Centroamérica', nos 20 and 21, December 1985 and June 1987.

Table 1.4: Central America: agricultural exports, 1977–85 ('000,000 Central American pesos)

	1977	1978	1979	1980	1981	1982	1983	1984	1985
Meat	136.30	213.50	293.10	222.30	174.10	154.60	122.80	86.10	91.40
Bananas	304.90	336.30	426.00	530.70	499.50	530.10	494.80	565.60	521.90
Sugar	158.40	105.40	129.60	178.50	218.10	89.60	204.40	129.70	69.40
Coffee	1821.80	1408.20	1674.70	1352.80	963.80	829.20	1043.20	1230.40	1278.90
Cotton	387.60	403.70	415.00	296.30	294.20	212.70	218.10	220.00	172.80
Total traditional products	**2809.00**	**2467.10**	**2938.40**	**2580.60**	**2149.70**	**1816.20**	**2083.30**	**2231.80**	**2134.40**
Cocoa	31.30	24.10	19.70	8.20	4.10	4.20	4.80	7.30	6.90
Tobacco	21.10	24.00	29.60	34.00	35.10	28.80	29.30	30.60	24.90
Wood	56.70	53.60	46.40	25.80	30.90	45.90	38.60	36.00	35.70
Plants, seeds, flowers, etc.	28.20	29.40	56.70	51.10	28.80	19.10	32.60	75.20	58.80
Total non-traditional products	**137.30**	**131.10**	**152.40**	**119.10**	**98.90**	**98.00**	**105.30**	**149.10**	**126.30**
Agricultural products	2946.30	2598.20	3090.80	2699.70	2248.60	1914.20	2188.60	2380.90	2260.70
Total exports	**4108.80**	**3855.40**	**4470.80**	**4444.60**	**3820.70**	**3423.40**	**3548.80**	**3544.80**	**3282.60**

SOURCE: As Table 1.3.

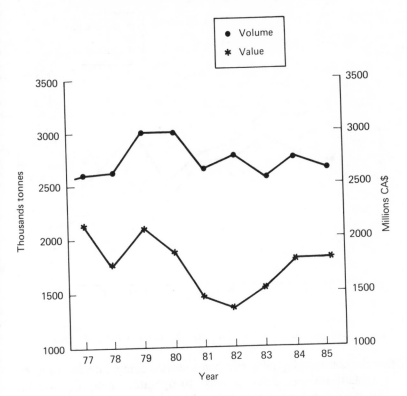

Figure 1.1 *Central American exports: coffee and bananas*

boom, each one of them in decline for various reasons, amongst which the political factor cannot be ignored. Even before policies against Nicaragua took a military turn the country was punished with the suppression of the North American quotas for beef and sugar; the trade embargo in its turn suspended all trade between both countries, badly affecting exports of coffee and cotton. Nicaragua was the least important banana country and the only foreign plantation in existence on the country's Atlantic coast was nationalised without trauma in 1981.

The fact that *the supply* of the three products which renewed regional export agriculture originates in developed economies has various consequences at a time of competition in a market in crisis. The first of these is that price formation is changed; in some cases, in favour of the society with the highest level of development of its productive forces, or in others, for the size of demand. The second is

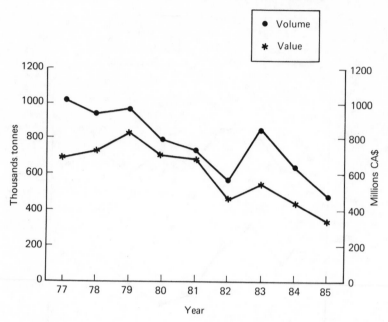

Figure 1.2   *Central American exports: sugar, meat and cotton*

that the commercial links based on so-called comparative advantages in agricultural specialisation cease to operate, simply because the crisis in foreign trade paralyses those fragile positive effects. Another effect, closer to common sense, is that the autonomy which a developed country has in market decisions, in comparison to that of its periphery, enables it to protect its internal market to the detriment of the external market and in violation of the GATT norms. It should not be forgotten that economic decisions always move along political tracks and are taken by politicians.

It is for that reason that we believe the greatest expression of dependency is the history of how the producers and exporters of cotton, sugar and meat were established and then how they went into crisis. Some things have already been said on this. Now it should be added that the crisis drastically affected production as well as sales of such products. The former because imported agro-industrial inputs were needed in abundance; the latter because they are inessential products. The crisis of cotton is taking place within the international fibre market with a strong fall in prices (including transport, insurance and so on); that of meat and sugar is within the North

American market, because the quotas given by that country's government tend to decrease in the face of strongly subsidised local producers. It is enough to say, for example, that in 1978 Central America exported US $722 million in meat, sugar and cotton and in 1985 US $333 million. Cotton took the highest share of the disaster, beginning a decline which still has not halted, followed by meat, which could be and has been substituted by North American producers for their own market. Apart from Nicaragua, the effects are almost the same in the other countries, but Costa Rica is better placed because it has never produced cotton and, despite everything, has managed to keep up its sales of meat abroad.

The decline of production/export has social and political effects which cannot be discussed here. The political crisis, defined as a massive and armed challenge to traditional power, began before the fall in exports, but the way in which the 'boom' started off and developed is present, without doubt, in the unfolding of that crisis. In other words, the form which modernisation took, as much as its stagnation, has contributed to the deep-seated troubles Central America is living through.

Each one of the three periods of the history of agro-exports in Central America brought misery and pain for the peasantry. No moment of bonanza in prices or expansion of profits translated into better standards of living. A new period of economic and political limits has fallen on the shoulders of the peasantry. In the intervening 25 years, the population doubled and production of basic grains was below that growth rate (see Figure 1.3). From the technical point of view, the decline in production is a function of the scarcity of land. Alongside it is the 'technical progress' of export agriculture from which food crops are excluded. In a society where some subsectors contribute efficiently to economic growth and others fall behind, the problem is not just technical but social. The poor performance of agriculture for popular consumption may not affect the problem of foreign exchange as such (through the need to import), as much as the availability of food. Rural poverty has visibly increased as a result.

There are other problems. Agro-industrial resources controlled by the large packers, the cotton gins and sugar mills, as well as the network of machinery (tractors, fumigation planes, transport equipment, and so on) and other inputs, have had to be abandoned or under-utilised. This mass of production goods are not only a sum of resources available to their owners, but are the expression of a

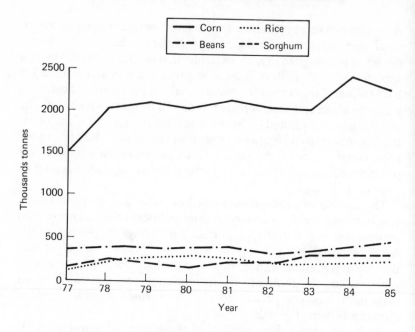

Figure 1.3   *Central America: production of basic grains*

national effort. The problem which they pose goes beyond the moment of the crisis and is linked to the very destiny of these agro-exporting societies.

Sugar will no longer be a product of international demand. The costs of production are now above external prices and those foreseeable in the future. It is only maintained because of the North American quota which 'will tend to disappear by the end of the present decade' (CEPAL, 1985:22). Besides, in the US they are beginning to substitute sugar for corn-honey on a much greater scale. Predictions for meat are less negative but will depend on the reactivation of the North American economy, which appears ever more like an engine ready gradually to shed its wagons. The powerful protectionism in the European Community and its abundant production of meat does not offer an appropriate outlet for Central American meat. But where the future is most in question is coffee, which is threatened not so much by the excess of future production as by a decrease in demand, originating in the search for less 'harmful' substitutes. The first of these was decaffeinated coffee. Now a new hot drink is under experiment and it is expected that at the beginning

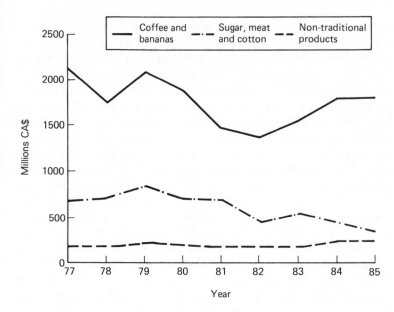

Figure 1.4   *Central America: value of agricultural exports*

of the next century coffee will cease to be a popular habit and become a vice of old nostalgics. Stress and caffeine are not compatible.

Generally, the weight of agricultural products in international trade has been in irreversible decline. The crisis of this decade has shown that when external demand is weakened it affects industrial products less (see Figure 1.4). In other words, and with respect to the last years, the rhythm of growth in world trade of agricultural products grew more than 4 per cent from 1960 to 1970, but only 1.3 per cent in 1979–86 (IICA, 1987). For Latin America growth was negative between 1982 and 1986. Prices for the fifteen main Latin American exports (including meat, cotton, sugar, banana and coffee) decreased between 25 and 60 per cent in the period cited (1981–6). At the same time, the most developed countries increased their participation in agricultural trade from 53 to 64 per cent (between 1960 and 1980) (IICA, 1987).

Finally, it would be useful to mention the hypothesis analysed by Bulmer-Thomas, who suggested that the participation of the agricultural sector in GDP must decline as *per capita* income increases. 'Such a decline', he suggests, 'can be explained in different ways, Engel's Law being one of the most persuasive. According to it, as income grows, the proportion spent on food decreases; it can be expected, therefore, that production from the agricultural sector increases less rapidly than GDP globally' (Bulmer-Thomas, 1983:275).[2] As discussed by Bulmer-Thomas in his important work, the decline of food production in total GDP is evident. In previous decades, *per capita* income increased, but there was a shift towards production to meet external demand at the expense of basic grain production. Nevertheless, in recent years there has been a recovery, which appears similar to that which arose in the years following the crisis of 1929–30. But the appearance is superficial. Today it is not the peasants who take refuge in their subsistence economies to reproduce their social existence by planting maize. These and other grains, as it appears from the analysis of Baumeister (1987:19–34), emerge as crops grown by a middle and large peasantry and, in any case, in new zones earlier dedicated to agro-export. It should not be forgotten that the use of the soil and the relationship of man to land changed brutally with the triple 'boom'. The best land was taken over and advances made into that of medium quality. Extensive cattle ranching came to occupy about two-thirds of the land of farms; 40 per cent of Central America's forests disappeared when their land was settled and put into use or left fallow to await a future which is vanishing.

4. THE FUTURE OF THE AGRO-EXPORT ECONOMY

The experience of more than a century of agricultural activity for export constitutes a contradictory puzzle when thinking about the future of Central American societies. On the one hand, neither agricultural growth by itself nor its diversification and modernisation were sufficient 'starting motors' to introduce necessary changes. These have not taken place, even at the greatest moments of the export boom. Nevertheless, there is a link between the growth of exports (the income of foreign exchange brought with it) and economic diversification into non-agricultural activities. One of the conditions for this to happen is the persistence of that other phenomenon, the vitality of the internal market and its demand. The links between internal accumulation and the dynamic of the world market must be specified, but they pass through the role of the state, business groups, foreign capital and so on; but especially through the weight of dominant economic interests.

In the present situation of crisis, Central America is making efforts

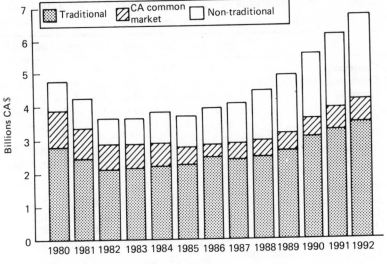

Figure 1.5 *Central American exports of basic products, 1980–92**

SOURCE: United States Department of State Agency for International Development (1987), *Report to the President and the Congress: A Plan for Fully Funding the Recommendations of the National Bipartism Commission on Central America*, special report no. 162 (Washington, D.C.: Department of State, Office of Management and Budget).

to diversify its exportable production. This includes the agricultural sector, divided into 'traditional' and 'non-traditional', but including now under the latter *everything* which did not form part of the export structure up to the 1980s (see Figure 1.5). These efforts show a number of characteristics. In the first place, there are primary products which, once more, respond to a cautious, slow external demand which is full of requirements: plants, ornamental flower seeds, flowers, shrimps, and so on (see Table 1.5). The supply from Central America faces administrative rules, not just commercial obstacles. There is no open competition but a market, such as the North American, which is usually closed and opened selectively. In the second place, no Central American state has managed to establish a coherent and dynamic policy, although steps have certainly been taken in that direction, particularly in Costa Rica and Guatemala. But these efforts are not based on products whose technical composition and value-added can

Table 1.5:   Non-traditional agricultural exports, 1978–85 ('000,000 Central American pesos)

	1978	1979	1980	1981	1982	1983	1984	1985
Guatemala								
Crustaceans and molluscs	7.9	6.1	8.8	7.1	11.2	9.6	12.6	10.0
Cocoa	7.6	0.9	0.3	0.6	0.0	1.9	2.7	0.8
Tobacco	10.8	13.1	16.3	16.0	12.9	13.7	17.4	13.5
Wood	0.4	0.9	0.3	0.3	2.2	1.1	1.4	2.5
Plants, seeds, flowers, and others	29.1	56.3	48.5	25.9	17.7	30.6	74.6	58.2
Total	**55.8**	**77.3**	**74.2**	**49.9**	**44.0**	**56.9**	**108.7**	**85.0**
El Salvador								
Crustaceans and molluscs	10.7	13.1	17.1	23.1	21.3	12.8	19.0	23.3
Cocoa	0.1	0.0	0.0	0.0	0.0	0.1	0.0	0.2
Tobacco	1.1	1.3	2.4	0.2	0.4	1.4	0.7	0.2
Wood	0.0	0.0	0.0	0.0	0.0	0.0	0.0	0.0
Plants, seeds, flowers, and others	0.0	0.0	0.0	0.0	0.0	0.0	0.0	0.0
Total	**11.9**	**14.4**	**19.5**	**23.3**	**21.7**	**14.3**	**19.7**	**23.7**
Honduras								
Crustaceans and molluscs	15.7	24.8	23.6	26.3	28.1	36.0	35.7	44.5
Cocoa	1.1	0.1	0.1	0.8	1.8	1.8	3.1	3.1
Tobacco	0.9	12.1	13.7	13.3	10.8	10.8	8.3	8.7
Wood	42.3	41.2	24.5	26.9	42.6	35.4	33.1	32.0
Plants, seeds, flowers, and others	0.0	0.1	0.2	1.8	0.3	0.0	0.0	0.0
Total	**60.0**	**78.3**	**62.1**	**69.1**	**83.6**	**84.0**	**80.2**	**88.3**
Costa Rica								
Crustaceans and molluscs	4.4	0.5	5.7	3.9	3.6	3.1	9.9	17.6
Cocoa	15.1	9.7	4.2	2.7	2.4	1.0	1.5	2.5
Tobacco	0.1	0.1	0.2	0.1	0.3	0.0	0.0	0.0
Wood	0.3	0.0	0.0	0.1	0.5	1.0	1.3	1.2
Plants, seeds, flowers, and others	0.2	0.3	0.4	1.0	1.1	1.0	0.5	0.6
Total	**20.1**	**10.6**	**10.5**	**7.8**	**7.9**	**6.1**	**13.2**	**21.9**
Nicaragua								
Crustaceans and molluscs	14.7	21.7	26.8	17.9	16.2	16.8	9.6	9.4
Cocoa	0.2	0.0	0.0	0.0	0.0	0.0	0.0	0.3
Tobacco	3.0	3.0	1.4	3.7	4.4	3.4	4.2	2.5
Wood	7.0	4.3	1.0	0.9	0.6	1.1	0.2	0.0
Plants, seeds, flowers, and others	0.1	0.0	0.2	0.1	0.0	1.0	0.1	0.0
Total	**25.0**	**29.0**	**29.4**	**22.6**	**21.2**	**22.3**	**14.1**	**12.2**

SOURCE: As Table 1.3.

Table 1.6: US imports of Central American horticultural products,[a]
1980–7 ('000,000 US $)

	1980	1981	1982	1983	1984	1985	1986	1987
Costa Rica								
Fruits and vegetables	5.3	5.9	6.7	8.9	10.8	11.9	20.8	26.9
Plants, flowers, etc.	8.1	5.8	6.3	6.1	11.0	12.0	13.1	15.2
Total	**13.4**	**11.7**	**13.0**	**15.0**	**21.8**	**23.9**	**33.9**	**42.1**
El Salvador								
Fruits and vegetables	1.8	0.8	1.6	1.6	2.4	3.3	4.8	5.9
Plants, flowers, etc.	1.5	1.2	1.0	0.7	0.8	0.6	0.5	0.9
Total	**3.3**	**2.0**	**2.6**	**2.3**	**3.2**	**3.9**	**5.3**	**6.8**
Guatemala								
Fruits and vegetables	5.5	8.0	10.9	10.0	13.2	15.0	18.4	27.2
Plants, flowers, etc.	6.5	7.3	7.0	6.1	8.2	8.2	8.2	9.9
Total	**12.0**	**15.3**	**17.9**	**16.1**	**21.4**	**23.2**	**26.6**	**37.1**
Honduras								
Fruits and vegetables	10.1	10.6	10.8	10.8	13.4	16.3	16.4	27.4
Plants, flowers, etc.	2.6	2.0	2.0	1.6	2.2	1.5	1.2	1.7
Total	**12.7**	**12.6**	**12.8**	**12.4**	**15.6**	**17.8**	**17.6**	**29.1**
Central America								
Fruits and vegetables	22.7	25.3	30.0	31.3	39.8	46.5	60.4	87.4
Plants, flowers, etc.	18.7	16.3	16.3	14.5	22.2	22.3	23.0	27.7
Total[b]	**41.4**	**41.6**	**46.3**	**45.8**	**62.0**	**68.8**	**83.4**	**115.1**

SOURCE: United States, Department of Commerce, unpublished information.

NOTES: [a] Excludes bananas.
[b] Excludes Nicaragua.

form a solid basis for a project of economic growth. In the third place, the policy to encourage non-traditional exports is promoted (inspiration, resources, managerial direction, and so on) directly by the US through the Agency for International Development (AID) substituting for the role previously played by the State (see Table 1.6).

The overall balance of these developments is not very positive. There is a general phenomenon of a historic character: the international economic crisis has already shown that in the coming period nothing will remain the same in world trade. Nor is it possible to hope – as in the past – for a take-off effect based on the recovery of dynamism by the central countries. The greatest threat of 'delinking', which appears inevitable, is associated with the historic trend of falling international demand for our 'traditional' products. Not only is the past trend one of decline, but the future is also discouraging (see Tables 1.3 and 1.4), as much a result of the relative decrease in the use of coffee or sugar as of competition from Africa, but especially from the large markets' tendency to protect themselves. Some commercial schemes occasionally stimulate policies of export diversification in Central America, such as the Caribbean Basin Initiative and some co-operation agreements with the EEC. But nothing will be sufficient if it does not count on strengthened international demand.

With it or without it, eyes must turn to the internal market and make part of the reactivation rest – in the medium turn, at least – on the dynamic of local demand. The use of the region's own natural resources can be the basis of a new stage of industrialisation, for export and for the moribund Regional Common Market, and also for the drive to achieve food self-sufficiency, at present ever more distant. For this and other measures which affect the future, not only is a common will needed to march forward, but also a climate of peace with social justice, only with that do we have national and future viability.

Notes

1. In Costa Rica, United Brands operates in Golfito and the other two in Limon; in Guatemala, only del Monte, in the region of Morales and in Honduras, United Brands in La Lima and Castle & Cooke in La Ceiba, changing the previous conditions of competition and percentage participation in the international market totally.
2. Already in 1947 Raul Prebisch had shown the truth of this trend. His proposals for industrialisation were based on the gradual loss of dynamism of the rural sector.

Bibliography

Baumeister, Eduardo (1987), *Tendencias de la Agricultura Centroamericana en los Años Ochenta*, Cuadernos de Ciencias Sociales (San José, Costa Rica: FLACSO).

Bulmer-Thomas, Victor (1983), 'Economic Development over the Long Run: Central America since 1920', *Journal of Latin American Studies*, vol. 15, part 2, pp. 269–94.

Bulmer-Thomas, Victor (1986), 'Cuentas Nacionales de Centroamérica desde 1920', in *Anuario de Estudios Centroamericanos*, vol. 12 (San José, Costa Rica: Universidad de Costa Rica).

CEPAL (1985), *Notas para el Estudio Económico de América Latina y el Caribe*, cited by Baumeister, op. cit.

CEPAL (1986), 'El Crecimiento Centroamericano en la Postguerra', in *Raíces y Perspectivas de la Crisis Económica* (San José: ICADIS), Serie Para Entender Centroamérica, no. 4.

Consejo Monetario Centroamericano (1987), *Situación Económica de los Países Centroamericanos en 1986* (Guatemala Ciudad: Consejo Monetario Centroamericano).

Ellis, Frank (1978), 'The Banana Export Activity in Central America in 1974–76; A Case Study of Plantation Exports by Vertically-Integrated Transnational Corporations' (D. Phil. thesis, Sussex University).

Gallardo, Ma. Eugenia and López, R. (1986), *Centroamérica: La Crisis en Cifras*, (San José, Costa Rica: FLACSO-IICA).

Instituto Interamericano de Cooperación Agrícola (IICA) (1987), *Perspectivas de la Agricultura en América Latina y el Caribe*, presented at the Conference on the World Production of Food, Madrid.

López, José Roberto (1986), *La Economía del Banano en Centroamérica* (San José, Costa Rica: DEI-FLACSO).

Paige, Jeffrey M. (1987), 'Coffee and Politics in Central America', in Richard Tardanico, *Crises in the Caribbean Basin* (London: Sage) p. 143.

SIECA-Agropecuaria 224 (1966), *El Algodón en Centroamérica* (Guatemala Ciudad: SIECA).

Torres-Rivas, Edelberto (1982), *El Desarrollo de la Agricultura en Centroamérica*, Documentos de Estudio (San José, Costa Rica: CSUCA). Mimeograph.

Torres-Rivas, Edelberto (1986), 'Cambios en la producción bananera en Honduras y Costa Rica: una aproximación estructural', in *Las Implicaciones socioeconómicas de los cambios estructurales en las plantaciones de América Latina* (Geneva, Switzerland: OIT).

Williams, Robert G. (1986), *Export Agriculture and the Crisis in Central America* (Chapel Hill, N.C.: University of North Carolina Press).

2 International Markets and Perspectives for Central American Traditional Exports: Coffee, Cotton and Bananas

Massimo Micarelli

Any recovery plan for the Central American economies must take into account the huge dependency on exports of green coffee, raw cotton and bananas. This analysis will outline the conditions of the world market for these exports, particularly in the European Economic Community (EEC). If Central American countries come out of the political crisis within a framework of peace, rapid economic recuperation will be needed, which will rely on traditional exports. In this chapter the main characteristics of the world markets and their long-run tendencies will be discussed, as well as trends in the 1980s. The evolution of prices for the three products will be a particularly important topic. The perspectives of the EEC markets will also be dealt with, with consideration of their generally oligopolistic nature. In the final part, some conclusions will be drawn and a comparative table is presented with the general outlook for the three principal traditional Central American export commodities.

1. WORLD MARKETS: MAIN ECONOMIC INDICATORS

Comparative analysis of the main economic indices for the three products gives a gloomy picture on average, particularly for the 1980s (see Table 2.1). The coffee market shows positive as well as negative trends, but nevertheless it is in a relatively better position than the two other commodities. The picture for bananas is slightly unfavour-

37

Table 2.1: Survey of trends of Central American traditional exports to international markets

Item	Bananas	(%)	Coffee	(%)	Cotton	(%)
World market						
1980–4						
Prices	Stable	+0.4	Declining	−1.1	Falling	−3.2
Exports	Declining	−1.3	Increase	+3.5	Declining	−2.5
Exp. gains	Small fluctuations	2.8	Great instability	21.8	Instability	4.6
Production	Stable	+0.6	Stable	+0.8	Increase	+4.3
Consumption	Stable	+0.1	Increase	+1.5	Small increase	+0.9
Stocks	None		High level	60.0	Very high level	100
Overall	Stable		Best + neg. elements		Gloomy	
1984–6						
Prices	30–45 $ cents/kg. Now low (35 cents) No agreement		100–215 $ cents/lb. CA gains 1986/loss 1987 ICO general + country quota, Fluct. band 140–120 $ cents/lb.		100–200 $ cents/lb. Now very low (100 $ cts) No agreement	
1982–6						
Growth	Consumption	+20.0			Production Exports Stocks	+21.7 +7.5 +103
1984–6						
Shares	Exp. CA/world	1/3	Prod. CA/World Imp. CA/USA Imp. CA/EEC	1/10 1/6 1/12	Prod. CA/World Exp. CA/World	1/100 1/30
Growth	Imports	+10.7				
Quality	Latin-Am. Standard Africa poor investments		Latin-Am. Arabica Africa/Asia Robusta		Depends on length of lint	

(continued on page 38)

Table 2.1: *continued*

Item	Bananas	(%)	Coffee	(%)	Cotton	(%)
EEC market						
1980–6						
Imports	Total From CA	+10.6 –8.2	Total From CA	+11.0 –22.0	Total From CA	+21.4 –76.0
Trade regime	Non-ACP duty + quotas Import stop Italy/France/UK	20.0	Non-ACP duty + levies	4.5	No duty	
1986						
Shares	CA/EEC imports Italy + W. Germany in EEC imp. CA 3 US TNC/worldtrade TNC/Italy trade TNC/France trade TNC/W. Germany trade Producer/final price	1/4 4/5 7/10 7/10 1/4 4/10 1/7	CA/EEC imports Italy + W. Germany in EEC imp. CA EEC-north: Arabica EEC-south: Robusta Producer/final price	1/11 2/3 4/5 1/2 1/3	CA/EEC imports Italy + W. Germany in EEC imp. CA	1/40 2/3
Degree of competition	France + UK: Ex-colonies. Inclusion Madeira + Canaries		W. Germany: oligopolistic Italy: 230,000 bars		W. Germany: merchant houses Italy: import agencies	
Policy recommendations	Reduce duties + levies. Lower TNC control		Joint advertising. Extra services to imp. Lower levies in Germany/Italy		Processing in the producer country. Develop local textile industry	

SOURCE: See analysis in text.

NOTES: CA Central America.
TNC Transnational companies.

Table 2.2: Bananas, cotton, coffee: world market long-term basic economic indicators

	Period	Bananas (%)	Cotton (%)	Coffee (%)
Current prices trend	1973–9	+11.4	+6.7	+24.6
	1980–6	−1.3	−7.8	+3.1
Consumption trend differences	1963–72/	−0.4	−0.9	−1.3
due to income effects	1973–84	−1.3	−1.2	−1.1
Growth value:				
Exports	1973–9	−2.2	−2.7	+4.2
	1980–4	−1.3	−2.5	+3.5
Production	1973–9	−2.4	+4.3	−0.9
	1980–4	0.6	+4.3	+0.8
Consumption	1973–9	−2.8	+0.4	+1.5
	1980–4	−0.5	+1.6	+1.7
Growth volume				
Exports	1980–4	−1.5	−3.9	+3.4
Production	1980–4	+0.3	+0.1	+0.8
LDC participation in world exports	1983–4	90	40	92
Instability of export gains	1962–71	4.4	4.4	5.3
	1972–84	2.8	4.6	21.8
Stocks in terms of consumption of				
developed countries	1980	—	55.4	59.0
	1984	—	103.7	69.1
Trend in:				
Crop areas	1962–84	—	+0.04	+0.13
Yield	1962–84	—	+0.82	+0.94

SOURCE: UNCTAD (1987), TD 328, 'Revitalising Development Growth and International Trade: Assessment and Policy Options – Addendum 3: Commodities', 27 February (Geneva).

able, but cotton is in the worst position. Table 2.2 give some long-term trends in the characteristics of the three markets.

Price tendencies in the 1980s are positive only for coffee, because of high increases that occurred in the 1985–6 market period, and in spite of a small drop between 1980–4. The banana market is more stable but shows a slight tendency to decline, Cotton prices drop regularly in this period. Export values have the same trends as their prices. The coffee market is broadening, while banana and cotton markets are narrowing in comparison with the 1970s when prices rose for all three, most strongly for coffee and less so for cotton.

Instability of export earnings, however, weakens the comfortable picture for coffee. The wide fluctuations of international market prices regularly hit coffee exports in the 1970s as well as in the 1980s, and more often than cotton and bananas. Instability of coffee and banana exports cannot be counterbalanced easily by Third World supply control, in spite of their high participation (about 90 per cent) in the market. In the cotton market, China has made a big effort to increase its share (a third of total world supply) and has lifted Third World supply participation from 40 per cent to 60 per cent between 1984 and 1986.

Production of coffee and banana crops grew slowly, particularly in the 1980s, while raw cotton production increased steadily from 1973 onwards (+4.3 per cent each year), in order to maintain export earnings at a time of declining world prices. Producers concentrated their efforts on yields, particularly in the 1960s. Coffee yields grew annually by 0.94 per cent and cotton by 0.82 per cent between 1962 and 1984, but these figures are well below those for grains, tea and sugar (see Table 2.2). Increases in world consumption were significant for coffee and cotton but its rates slackened more and more in the 1970s as well as in the 1980s. Banana consumption decreased steadily in both periods. The main reason for these trends can be found in the general decrease of world growth rates. Decreasing consumption in the developed countries is rather critical for cotton (−1.2 per cent and −1 per cent in 1963–72 and 1973–84), while coffee and bananas maintained their very low rate of consumption growth in developed countries (an average of 0.9 per cent and 0.5 per cent respectively between 1973 and 1984: see Table 2.3).

Finally, stock levels are a heavy burden for cotton producers (103 per cent of the world consumption in 1984). Cotton and coffee have always had the highest stock levels compared to consumption of all primary agricultural commodities. Bananas have a very rapid consumption time, about one month from their harvest, so that stocks cannot be high.

A general comparison of the last twenty years can be made on the basis of the six trends mentioned. The clearest picture can be seen in coffee: prices, exports and consumption have positive long-term trends, almost completely counterbalanced by the high instability of export earnings, stocks and poor trends in the growth of production. If we pay attention to the generally gloomy trend for all agricultural exports in the 1980s, coffee shows a relatively good picture. On the other hand, bananas and cotton were more seriously affected by the

Table 2.3: Coffee, cotton and bananas: world imports, 1975, 1980, 1984 (millions US$/1000 metric tonnes, percentages)

	Coffee								Cotton								Bananas							
	Million $			000/t			%		Million $			000/t			%		Million $			000/t			%	
	1975	1980	1984	1975	1980	1984	1980	1984	1975	1980	1984	1975	1980	1984	1980	1984	1975	1980	1984	1975	1980	1984	1980	1984
World	4980	14080	11504	3679	3797	4958	100.0	100.0	4939	8785	7598	4084	5070	4435	100.0	100.0	1374	2162	2240	6309	6765	6597	100.0	100.0
DC	4364	12302	10277	3197	3310	3451	87.2	85.0	2218	3628	3501	1876	1948	1923	38.4	43.3	1169	1813	1981	5352	5590	5808	82.6	88.0
USA	1587	3945	3115	1394	1107	1080	29.1	26.6	14	3	8	11	3	5	0.0	0.0	230	429	650	1967	2423	2665	35.8	40.4
EEC	1930	5857	5006	1392	1573	1656	41.4	40.8	1192	1947	1826	1023	1049	1014	20.7	22.6	616	939	825	1946	1877	1859	27.7	28.2
France	382	1168	922	295	327	306	8.6	7.5	233	334	276	214	196	165	3.9	3.7	194	241	203	478	446	443	6.6	6.7
West Germany	538	1741	1577	373	468	516	12.3	12.7	251	352	372	228	193	212	3.8	4.8	152	267	241	548	534	549	7.9	8.3
Italy	275	830	657	202	221	225	5.8	5.5	240	479	492	195	252	257	5.0	5.8	91	130	123	304	279	315	4.1	4.8
United Kingdom	113	274	361	93	74	116	1.9	2.8	132	131	88	113	69	48	1.4	1.1	102	174	162	308	232	309	4.8	4.7
Japan	152	669	687	110	175	223	4.6	5.5	827	1346	1299	692	719	708	14.2	16.0	163	192	256	894	726	682	10.7	10.3
LDC	359	927	698	277	254	347	6.7	8.5	1359	2348	2684	1215	1411	1614	27.8	36.4	154	274	211	679	906	629	13.4	9.5

SOURCE: UNCTAD (1986), *Commodity Yearbook* (Geneva: UNCTAD).

crisis: the former suffered a modest deterioration in prices, exports, production and consumption; while the latter was hit more and more by a steady fall in prices, exports and large stocks without counter-balancing increases in production and consumption.

Differences in the qualities of the three products are particularly important for the coffee market. Latin American producers harvest mainly 'Arabica' and within this 'Other Milds' qualities, but African and Asian producers harvest 'Robusta' quality, which is cheaper. Coffee consumption is a mixture of many qualities. 'Arabica' is usually the more consistent component, but there is often a higher percentage of 'Robusta' added. 'Other Milds' are utilised in small percentages and are particularly important in the bar blends; this coffee grows on the highlands of Colombia, Central America, Kenya and India. Cotton has different qualities too, but they are not so typical of any region or country. Better quality mainly relies on length of the lint, because the longer it is, the less spinners have to twist in the elaboration of cotton yarns, thus lowering processing costs.

The market for bananas does not have these kinds of quality differences, because crops have been standardised for a long time by multinational companies, particularly in Latin America. Lower quality in African banana crops is generally caused by poor investment in production processes and organisation, which is often inherited from colonial times when there was a guarantee of export demand by a monopolist regime.

In terms of trade regimes, developed countries have different customs duties for our three products. Coffee is duty-free in the USA and Japan but the EEC maintains a 4.5 per cent customs duty 'ad valorem' on non-ACP exports. Moreover, in the EEC there are different taxes on consumption and value-added, which are particularly high in the main importing countries, Italy and Germany. Raw cotton has no duties in the EEC, but bananas from non-ACP exporters are subject to a 20 per cent duty plus a system of different quotas in each EEC member country. These barriers safeguard ACP traditional exports, mainly from African and Caribbean ex-colonies of France and Great Britain. Italy would like to protect Somalia exports, but their small quantity meets only 10 per cent of demand. In 1987 France, Italy and Great Britain announced a temporary suspension of imports from non-ACP countries, so that Central American exports have been substituted by ACP supplies.[1] The international banana market has always been controlled by three big transnational companies (TNCs): United Brands (30 per cent in 1981), Standard

Fruit (25 per cent), Del Monte (15 per cent). Recently a private Ecuadorian group, Noboa, entered the family of biggest traders. The big three North American TNCs controlled 70 per cent of the world market in 1981 and 100 per cent of Central American exports.[2] TNCs controlled Central American production directly or indirectly by agreements arranged with local producers, who are fully dependent on technology, infrastructure and the trade organisation of the same TNCs, which have been in operation since the Second World War.

2.   TRENDS IN THE 1980s

Bananas recovered their market in 1984–6. World imports grew by 10.7 per cent over the same period (7.4 million tons versus 6.7 million tons), exceeding the record level of 1979.[3] The four Central American exporting countries together (Costa Rica, Guatemala, Honduras and Nicaragua) shared about a third of the world market. Honduras and Costa Rica are considered among the biggest world exporters (12–14 per cent each), together with Colombia, Ecuador and the Philippines. Between 1982 and 1986 world consumption grew by about 20 per cent; whereas the United States has maintained its 37 per cent share and the EEC (10 countries) increased its share to 26.3 per cent of global banana consumption. The relevance of the US market is also shown by the high *per capita* yearly consumption (11.4 kg.), while in the EEC the average is 7.5 kg., but this figure was 8 kg. in 1973, decreased to 6.8 kg. in 1980 and started to increase again in the late 1980s.[4]

Cotton production and exports on a global scale have been growing during the 1980s (see Table 2.4). Production grew by 21.7 per cent and exports by 7.5 per cent from 1980 to 1986, but stocks, unfortunately, doubled in the same period and imports remained roughly unchanged. Four big producers (USA, USSR, China and India) controlled 70 per cent of the production but only 40 per cent of the exports in 1986. China became the largest producer, but the poor trend of prices in the world market depressed its exports; this brought about a huge upsurge in its stocks (42.5 per cent of world stocks in 1986). Almost half of the imports are from the Eastern market, feeding the development of textile industries in Asian countries. The United States market is self-sufficient and the EEC maintains a limited share of world imports (18 per cent) in spite of the increase between 1980 and 1986. Central American production and exports

Table 2.4: Cotton: production, exports, imports and stocks, 1980–6 ('000t. and percentages)

Exporting countries	Production				Exports				Stocks				Importing countries	Imports			
	'000t		%		'000t		%		'000t		%			'000t		%	
	1980–1	1985–6	1980–1	1985–6	1980–1	1985–6	1980–1	1985–6	1980–1	1985–6	1980–1	1985–6		1980–1	1985–6	1980–1	1985–6
World	14472	17613	100.0	100.0	4292	4615	100.0	100.0	4614	9273	100.0	100.0	World	4484	4512	100.0	100.0
USA	2428	2973	17.0	16.9	1290	762	30.0	16.5	581	887	12.6	9.5	EEC	678	823	15.1	18.2
USSR	3079	2722	21.6	15.4	932	762	21.7	16.5	617	929	13.4	10.0	France	167	170	3.7	3.7
India	1336	1579	9.4	9.0	113	65	2.6	1.4	315	421	6.8	4.5	Germany	158	239	3.5	5.3
China	2710	5008	19.0	28.4	–	261	–	5.6	830	3939	18.0	42.5	UK	43	48	0.9	1.1
Pakistan	716	827	5.0	4.7	328	305	7.6	6.6	52	253	1.1	2.7	Italy	190	261	4.2	5.8
Egypt	529	458	3.7	2.6	157	174	3.6	3.8	61	84	1.3	0.9	Asia	2578	2143	57.5	47.5
Sudan	99	191	0.7	1.1	87	218	2.0	4.7	47	170	1.0	1.8	Japan	698	729	15.5	16.1
Turkey	484	565	3.4	3.2	228	174	5.3	3.8	108	170	2.3	1.8	China	737	22	16.4	0.5
Brazil	622	625	4.3	3.5	13	283	0.3	6.1	366	624	7.9	6.7	S. Korea	332	359	7.4	7.9
Salvador	43	16	0.3	0.1	30	22	0.7	0.5					Taiwan	214	287	4.8	6.4
Guatemala	126	71	0.9	0.4	108	50	2.5	1.1	n.a.				Hongkong	154	200	3.4	4.4
Nicaragua	75	71	0.5	0.4	67	76	1.5	1.6					Indonesia	102	114	2.3	2.5

SOURCE: International Cotton Advisory Committee (1987), *Cotton: World Statistics* (Washington, D.C.: Secretariat of ICAC) pp 18–25.

are very small. Production decreased in the 1980s from 1.7 per cent (El Salvador, Guatemala and Nicaragua together) to 0.9 per cent, while their exports decreased from 4.7 per cent to 3.2 per cent of the world total in the same period.

Coffee production went through a crisis during 1985–6, when Brazilian drought and subsequent speculation on the world market increased prices until mid-1986. Since the suspension of the ICO (International Coffee Organisation) agreement in February 1986, prices have been steadily decreasing, because supply is well in excess of demand. World production and exports are concentrated in a few countries like Brazil and Colombia with a combined share of about 40 per cent, Central America with 11 per cent (five countries), and so on. From the point of view of the importers, the EEC covers around half of world consumption, USA about a third, Japan 7 per cent and centrally planned economies only 2 per cent. However, the EEC is the principal market for African coffee and imports only 8 per cent of its demand from Central America.

The scale of the three world export markets measured in current values are quite different: coffee accounts for $12 billion, cotton for $7.5 billion and bananas only for $2 billion. Until June 1987 (nine months from October 1986), the global volume of coffee exports was well below the figure for 1984 (about 51 million bags of 60 kg. each, in 1987 it was 48.5 million bags).[5] Brazil recovered its exports in 1987 but remains below the 1981–2 record (13 million bags compared with 11 million in 1987). Colombia and 'Other Milds Arabica' producers recovered too, covering about half of world exports and maintained this share, substituting Brazilian losses after its drought. 'Robusta' producers, mainly in Africa, were affected by declining exports in 1987 (10 million bags compared with 12 million on average over the previous five years).[6]

3. PRICES

Prices of the three products have shown different trends in the 1980s (see Table 2.5). Latin American banana prices declined steadily in the 1980s and those of cotton too, particularly in 1986. Coffee prices rose in 1985–6 but dropped again in 1987. There is a 30–40 per cent difference in value per unit between the most expensive 'Colombia' and the cheapest 'Robusta' quality. Central American qualities, 'Other Milds', stay in the middle of the range. The economic

Table 2.5: Quarterly world market prices of bananas, coffee and cotton
(in current value), 1981–6

Year		Bananas	Coffee				Cotton
		Latin America	Brazil	Colombia	Guatemala	Other Milds	US
				(US cents/kg.)			
1981	I	42.7	485.0	n.a.	286.5	258.2	200.7
	II	42.1	361.8	300.8	273.5	224.5	188.9
	III	35.7	269.3	322.6	264.8	196.8	163.3
	IV	40.0	317.4	337.0	307.4	227.0	144.9
1982	I	41.0	306.4	339.8	313.5	245.8	138.1
	II	43.8	319.1	330.0	313.1	229.9	143.6
	III	32.6	319.7	314.5	306.2	231.8	152.9
	IV	32.3	302.2	326.2	302.1	272.4	145.1
1983	I	37.5	293.2	311.5	278.0	269.4	145.5
	II	51.3	310.4	300.8	278.1	267.2	157.2
	III	46.2	307.0	299.8	286.4	267.5	164.3
	IV	37.0	327.0	320.1	318.5	290.2	198.5
1984	I	39.1	341.5	329.6	321.2	301.5	176.0
	II	43.3	327.4	334.0	328.3	313.9	183.0
	III	36.2	330.1	323.5	315.9	309.0	155.0
	IV	29.2	322.0	312.0	306.5	293.6	147.9
1985	I	42.4	341.7	324.7	276.7	316.4	144.2
	II	44.1	313.7	322.9	268.4	311.4	140.8
	III	36.6	296.2	325.3	234.6	294.2	138.5
	IV	28.9	386.7	382.5	286.8	362.4	140.3
1986	I	40.6	636.7	562.1	368.2	518.6	140.7
	II	46.7	586.3	510.6	312.4	451.5	120.0
	III	36.7	429.3	438.4	311.9	401.1	68.9
	IV	35.8	386.5	429.3	205.4	345.8	106.9

SOURCE: IDB (1987), *Economic and Social Progress in Latin America* (Washington, D.C.: IDB) p. 474.

dependency of Central America on exports of these products is well known. Since the 1970s the five Central American countries have been gaining more than half their export income from three products (see Table 2.6). For Guatemala the share has been about 40 per cent, El Salvador and Nicaragua about 60 per cent, while the figures for Costa Rica and Honduras are somewhere between these two extremes. The coffee price skyrocketed in 1986, increasing the export dependency of the countries even more (see Table 2.6).

Table 2.6: Central America: bananas, coffee, cotton as percentage of total exports, 1972–86

	Costa Rica			El Salvador			Guatemala			Honduras			Nicaragua		
	1972–6	1981–5	1986	1972–6	1981–5	1986	1972–6	1981–5	1986	1972–6	1981–5	1986	1972–6	1981–5	1986
Bananas	24.8	24.2	17.1	—	—	—	—	—	—	26.1	30.2	39.0	—	—	—
Coffee	25.5	27.6	31.2	41.9	58.2	81.3	29.8	30.8	40.4	18.5	22.4	28.2	15.9	31.1	46.0
Cotton	—	—	—	10.7	5.6	5.4	11.3	7.6	6.9	—	—	—	26.8	26.3	31.2
Total commodities	**50.3**	**51.8**	**48.3**	**52.6**	**63.8**	**86.7**	**41.1**	**38.4**	**47.3**	**44.6**	**52.6**	**67.2**	**42.7**	**57.4**	**77.2**

SOURCE: IDB (1987), *Economic and Social Progress in Latin America* (Washington, D.C.: IDB) pp. 475, 476.

The coffee market is the only one ruled by an international agreement between producers and consumers. Since 1962 five agreements have somehow improved world trade conditions and price stability, but a yearly quota for almost all producers and a fluctuation band of prices (120–140 US cents/lb.) were only fixed in 1983. Fifty producing countries (95 per cent of world production) and 25 consuming countries (developed economies, excluding the centrally planned ones) drafted and signed the agreement. The international price indicator is an average of prices of different qualities.

On 19 February 1986, after a great decrease in supply, prices rose for 45 days and after this period the ICO system of coffee quotas was suspended. When prices rise over 140 cents/lb., the International Coffee Organisation (ICO) permits producers to export more, enlarging general quotas and supply to satisfy the demand so that prices can fall. Coffee prices reached their top level in March 1986 (215 cents/lb.) because the market was afraid of a sudden shortage of the product. Moreover, the drought in Brazil reduced exports to about 10 million bags in 1985 (from 19.9 million bags in 1984). Importers increased their stocks of coffee and prices rose. After February 1987 prices decreased to about $1/lb. and were well below the established fluctuation band. Negotiations between producers and consumers brought about a new agreement in September 1987. New quotas were fixed for the next three months as consumers required, but in future quotas will probably also be arranged on the basis of the level of real production and stocks at that moment, as consumers wanted. This compromise maintains Brazil's leading role and gives limited satisfaction to other big exporters, such as Colombia and some Central American countries, but leaves a producer like Indonesia completely unsatisfied. The low price is now near the bottom line of the price fluctuation band. Central American countries lost about US $800 million in the 1987 export drive compared to 1986 when they had gained $300 million more than in the previous year.[7]

Finally, we can emphasise the difficulties in reaching international agreements on cotton and bananas. Third World producers control only 40 per cent of cotton exports and consumers will neither agree any economic measure to safeguard prices, nor will they accept management of world stocks and quotas by an international organisation. Bananas, with similar constraints, have the additional difficulties of inability to maintain stocks because this product is perishable, and also the problem of a few transnational companies controlling extensive parts of the world market.

4. EEC MARKETS

Imports of bananas into the EEC increased by 10.6 per cent during 1980–6, but the Central American quota decreased by 40,000 metric tonnes, from 28.6 per cent to 23.9 per cent of the total (see Table 2.7). French imports from the region practically disappeared (−45,000 tonnes) and in Germany it lost 20,000 tonnes in this period. Italy remains the most important market for Central American bananas (167,000 tonnes in 1986, 55 per cent of the volume of all Italian banana imports).

As mentioned earlier, in Italy imports from non-ACP countries were suspended, as well as in France and the UK, up to June 1988. Each EEC country has a yearly import quota of bananas, while in Italy and France monthly quotas are also provided. Such a high level of protection is unfair for non-ACP producers. But in Italy there is also a high level of duty on consumption (525 liras/kg.) which means that levies account for about 40 per cent of the retail price of bananas. In West Germany these taxes are not charged and there is a significant flow of re-exports to the other EEC members and North European countries. The protectionist attitude in Italy is due in part to such re-exports from West Germany, but is mainly due to the restriction of the consumption of tropical fruits which compete with national fruit production.

US transnationals control the market for bananas: 89 per cent in the USA, 71 per cent in Italy, 76 per cent in Japan, but also 43 per cent in West Germany and 24 per cent in France in 1980–1.[8] At that time, gross income shares were distributed as follows: only 14 per cent to the producer country, 16 per cent to freights and insurance, 21 per cent to ripeners in the importing country, 35 per cent to retailers and 13 per cent to other costs.[9]

Germany and Italy absorb about 80 per cent of the EEC banana imports from Central America, particularly from Honduras and Costa Rica which together provide 30 per cent of West German imports and 48 per cent of Italian imports. Apparent *per capita* consumption is very high in West Germany and comparable to the US (respectively 10 kg. and 11 kg. per year), but in Italy and the UK the *per capita* yearly figures are about 6 kg., well below the EEC average.

It is important to remember that in 1973, Costa Rica exported 480,000 tonnes of bananas to the EEC market, twice its present level. Central American exports are now also hit by the recent member-

Table 2.7: Bananas, coffee and cotton: EEC imports from Central America, 1980–6 ('000t. and percentages)

	EEC (10) '000t.		%		West Germany '000t.		%		France '000t.		%		Italy '000t.		%		United Kingdom '000t.		%	
	1980	1986	1980	1986	1980	1986	1980	1986	1980	1986	1980	1986	1980	1986	1980	1986	1980	1986	1980	1986
Bananas	1806.2	1999.3	100.0	100.0	518.9	656.9	100.0	100.0	445.9	453.0	100.0	100.0	279.0	299.8	100.0	100.0	293.8	318.5	100.0	100.0
Guatemala	54.2	28.1	3.0	1.4	6.4	3.0	1.2	0.5	12.0	—	2.7	—	25.7	23.8	9.2	7.9	2.7	1.2	0.9	0.4
Honduras	166.0	172.1	9.2	8.6	105.9	70.4	20.4	10.7	4.1	5.1	0.9	1.1	10.3	78.2	3.7	26.1	6.7	3.4	2.3	1.1
Nicaragua	—	42.7	—	2.1	—	17.9	—	2.7	—	1.0	—	0.2	—	0.2	—	—	—	—	—	—
Costa Rica	296.6	234.3	16.4	11.7	126.7	126.5	24.4	19.2	40.4	3.4	9.1	0.7	73.3	65.0	26.3	21.7	19.2	2.8	6.5	0.9
Central America	516.8	477.2	28.6	23.9	239.0	217.9	46.1	33.2	56.5	9.5	12.7	2.1	109.3	167.2	39.2	55.8	28.6	7.4	9.7	2.3
Coffee	1321.2	1470.7	100.0	100.0	463.5	566.6	100.0	100.0	302.2	259.8	100.0	100.0	219.8	251.3	100.0	100.0	71.0	98.1	100.0	100.0
Guatemala	39.4	28.9	3.0	2.0	20.9	11.8	4.5	2.1	2.9	2.5	1.0	1.0	4.6	7.4	2.1	2.9	1.6	1.9	2.2	1.9
Honduras	13.0	15.0	1.0	1.0	9.8	3.5	2.1	0.6	1.0	2.0	0.3	0.8	0.4	6.7	0.2	2.7	0.6	0.8	0.8	0.8
Salvador	76.7	40.3	5.8	2.7	55.8	31.6	12.1	5.6	2.7	4.0	0.9	1.5	2.2	0.8	1.0	0.3	0.7	—	0.9	—
Nicaragua	20.8	18.7	1.6	1.3	20.7	5.5	4.5	1.0	2.6	4.9	0.9	1.9	3.4	2.3	1.6	0.9	0.1	—	0.1	—
Costa Rica	25.8	33.1	1.9	2.2	13.3	13.1	2.9	2.3	4.5	3.7	1.5	1.4	3.3	4.4	1.5	1.7	0.8	9.7	1.2	9.9
Central America	175.7	136.0	13.3	9.2	120.5	65.4	26.0	11.5	13.7	17.1	4.5	6.6	13.9	21.6	6.3	8.6	3.8	12.4	5.3	12.6
Cotton	677.1	789.6	100.0	100.0	192.8	227.8	100.0	100.0	188.4	151.2	100.0	100.0	249.3	260.6	100.0	100.0	—	50.3	100.0	100.0
Guatemala	54.5	13.6	8.0	1.7	12.3	3.7	6.4	1.6	1.5	0.3	0.8	0.2	40.7	9.5	16.3	3.6	—	—	—	—
Salvador	12.9	2.1	1.9	0.3	1.3	1.3	0.7	0.6	6.2	0.4	3.3	0.3	5.3	0.2	2.1	0.1	—	—	—	—
Nicaragua	12.1	4.9	1.8	0.6	2.3	2.9	1.2	1.3	7.3	1.3	3.9	0.8	2.6	0.5	1.0	0.2	—	—	—	—
Central America	79.5	20.6	11.7	2.6	15.9	7.9	8.3	3.5	15.0	2.0	8.0	1.3	48.6	10.2	19.4	3.9	—	—	—	—

SOURCE: Nimexe, *Eurostat, 1980–86* (Luxemburg: European Community).

ships of Spain and Portugal. Their Atlantic islands, Madeira and the Canaries, add 450,000 tonnes to the EEC imports of bananas. Only half of EEC imports is allowed to come from non-ACP countries without duties. There is some pressure on the EEC to decrease its protectionist measures, but on the other hand, the preferential regime is essential for ACP exports. French and British interests would like to keep their ex-colonial partners in the banana trade. In evaluating these preferential relations, one must keep in mind that often quality, production and organisation in ACP countries are well below the standards of banana production of United States TNCs in Latin American countries.

In the EEC cotton market, Italy leads with a share of 5.8 per cent of the world imports in 1985–6; West Germany follows closely with 5.3 per cent. These two countries control about two-thirds of EEC imports, while France and the UK together account for about a quarter. Unfortunately, Central American cotton decreased its share of EEC imports from 11.7 per cent to 2.6 per cent between 1980 and 1986. The organisation of the cotton trade in the major importers, Italy and West Germany, is quite different: the former has several importing agencies, which are related directly to the spinners, while the latter has a small number of merchant houses which import raw cotton, select the various qualities and afterwards sell them to the spinners. This difference is typical of the Italian and West German markets for imported primary commodities. In West Germany there is a more complete and integrated structure than in Italy: oligopolistic wholesale organisations with big traders, some of them re-exporting to the rest of the EEC. There are also a small number of big industrial processors of the commodity and a significant vertical integration with the retailing market.

In the coffee market this structure is quite evident. In West Germany, there are three big roasting companies with a total market share of 51 per cent selling only to the wholesalers; two other big roasting companies (together controlling 34 per cent of the market) have their own *cafetarias* or coffee shops. In Italy, there are 1800 roasting companies, about 50 traders and 200 importing-and-roasting companies. These roasting companies sell 75 per cent of the roasted coffee to the retailers and 25 per cent to the bars.[10] There are 230,000 bars in Italy (a quarter of all retailers) in comparison with France where there are only 30,000. These Italian bars often depend on the roasting houses, which support the retail structure with equipment and credits. About 30–50 per cent of the coffee retail price is industrial value-added in West Germany and France, where the fluctuations of the international coffee market are transferred to consumer prices. In Italy, prices are more stable but are slowly increasing and the level of retail prices is three times that of import prices.[11] North European countries consume mainly Arabica (80 per cent), while Southern Europe uses between 40–60 per cent Robusta. *Per capita* consumption is high in West Germany (7 kg. annually) whereas in Italy consumption is only about 4 kg. and in Great Britain this figure is even lower. Great Britain and France have a significant consumption also of soluble coffee.

We can draw some conclusions from our analysis, looking at the future prospects for Central American exports of the three traditional commodities in the EEC market. To facilitate comparison we summarised in Table 2.1 some of the main issues of the current situation for each of the products dealt with in this chapter.

The best prospect seems to be in the coffee market: production, exports and consumption have positive outlooks, in spite of the recent world market price which is now below the intervention band. Central American producers can, in the short run, recover and perhaps improve their EEC market participation in two ways:

(a)   by stimulating market advertising, particularly in Italy and West Germany, through a joint campaign with roasting houses which sell bar blends;
(b)   by enriching just a little the quality of their supply through some export services, as required by bar retailers, particularly in Italy (green coffee without impurities, special bags, standard quality, and so on).

There might still exist some margin for increasing coffee consumption in countries like Great Britain and even Italy and France for the 'Other Milds' quality of Central America.

Central American exporters should adapt their strategy according to the different structures of the marketing organisations and roasting industries in the different countries of the EEC. Consumption levies and value-added taxes for coffee can be reduced in Italy and West Germany in the medium term, as well as the EEC external custom duties.

In the banana market, high customs duties and consumption levies are a colonial heritage. They could be reduced if ACP exports were safeguarded by realistic quotas. Unfortunately, for this product it is very difficult to bypass TNC control of production and the market, but in the northern countries of Europe something could be done.

The cotton market shows the gloomiest outlook for Central America. It seems as if production could be better utilised to supply the local textile industries, or the cotton land be reconverted to basic food crops, as is occurring in Nicaragua and Guatemala to some extent. For all three products Central American exporters must be considered as price takers.

Finally, mention should be made of the general slow-down in prices of primary commodities in dollar terms, due, among other things, to the US dollar devaluation. International prices of the three commodities are quoted in dollars and a 30 per cent devaluation, as happened in 1986–8 in terms of the EEC main currencies, will be a serious obstacle to the recovery of Central American real terms of trade.

Notes

1. *Telex Développement* (1987), 8 January; 14 March; 8 July.
2. J. R. Lopez (1986), *La Economia del Banano en Centro América* (San José, Costa Rica: DEI).
3. *Marchés Tropicaux* (1987), 7 August, p. 2145.
4. Ibid., p. 2146.
5. Ibid., 31 August, p. 2094.
6. Ibid.
7. *Latin America Economic Report* (1987), January, p. 14; and *Latin America Weekly Report*, 5 February, p. 8.
8. J. R. Lopez, op. cit., p. 147.
9. N. Girvan (1987), 'Transnational Corporation and Non-Fuel Primary Commodities in Developing Countries', *World Development*, no. 5, pp. 713–40.
10. *Marchés Tropicaux* (1987), 19 June, p. 1665.
11. *Largo Consumo* (1987), no. 5, p. 44 (special edition on coffee).

3 Selected Problems of the EEC Market for Central American Coffee

Elmar Meister

1. INTRODUCTION

This study focuses on two issues of special relevance to Central American coffee exports to the EEC. The first concerns the West German market, which is the most important market in Europe. Attention will mostly be drawn to the process of concentration in the processing industry and to the distribution of surplus profits of the coffee trade, a result of the very different positions of the competitors in this market. The second issue concerns European tariff preferences and their possible consequences, one of which is the shift of the regional origin of European coffee imports and the other is the disadvantages arising from a higher degree of processing of the commodity.

Coffee occupies thirtieth position in world trade, behind various industrial products such as cars, trucks, aeroplanes and their equipment, crude oil, gas, paper and steel, but also behind agricultural products such as wheat and meat. But its share is declining.[1] However, in value it is, after crude oil, the most important commodity of the developing countries, almost exclusively produced and exported by them.

Coffee owes its outstanding importance to the developing countries to two characteristics: first, it can be produced in tropical climates only, that is, the cultivation of the raw commodity is limited monopolistically to the tropical developing countries. Secondly, its production, especially harvesting, can be mechanised or industrialised only to a limited extent. Coffee is a labour-intensive product; cost reduction through technical advance is limited. Because of this, and in contrast to other agricultural commodities which are subject to competition from industrialised production, the production of coffee is relatively profitable, even in traditional or smallholder production.

54

On the other hand, with few appropriate or socially acceptable alternatives for diversification this causes worldwide overproduction and a continuous pressure on prices.

The world harvest is gathered in more than 70 developing countries. Nearly 20 million people are employed in the production, processing, transport and distribution of coffee. This gives a livelihood to 100 million people. From 1980 to 1984 the four biggest exporting countries alone represented 48.69 per cent of the world exports (Brazil 21.95 per cent, Colombia 16.98 per cent, Ivory Coast 5.29 per cent, Indonesia 4.47 per cent); the four main importers represented 58.12 per cent of all world imports (USA 29.31 per cent, West Germany 14.29 per cent, France 8.42 per cent, Italy 6.19 per cent).[2]

2. COFFEE IN WEST GERMANY

2.1 The Market

The ten EEC countries share 41.16 per cent (average value of imports in US$, 1980–4) of world imports and represent the main bloc of demand in the world market. West Germany is the most important market in the EEC, with an average of 14.29 per cent, representing 8.5 million bags, approximately DM4.4 billion in value in 1984.[3] In the world market it ranks second behind the USA. Because of intermediate and transit trade and the export of processed products, the EEC is also an increasing supplier, with a 4.6 per cent share of world coffee exports in 1980–4. During this period West Germany supplied 2.08 per cent of the world market. Since 1983 it has exceeded the export share of the USA. Due to the higher share of processed products it also exceeds, with the exception of Guatemala and El Salvador, any other Central American exporter in terms of value of exports.

In 1986 the total imports of West Germany in all forms of coffee amounted to 10.1 million bags green coffee equivalent.[4] Of these, 93.4 per cent were green coffee with caffeine and 0.22 per cent decaffeinated, 0.82 per cent roasted coffee, 0.02 per cent without caffeine and 5.53 per cent extracts in liquid or solid form. Overall, 2.9 million bags (29 per cent of total imports) were re-exported, 93.6 per cent in processed forms.

Of the whole volume of processed coffee in West Germany, 89 per cent was transformed into roasted coffee, 11 per cent decaffeinated, and 10 per cent was transformed into soluble coffee. The ever-increasing proportion of processed exports reveals the growing importance of the German coffee industry as a processor, mainly for its European neighbours. West Germany is the most important producer of roasted coffee in the EEC, followed by France, Italy and The Netherlands. At the same time, it is the world's most important producer of extracts, the only significant producer of this coffee form within the EEC.[5]

However, West Germany ranks midway in terms of its *per capita* coffee consumption of 6.86 kg. Consumption in Scandinavian countries is higher than 10 kg. *per capita*, in France it falls to 5.49 kg. and in the USA it is stagnant at approximately 4.65 kg.[6] There are two peculiarities in the German national market. The first is the state tax on coffee, which is the highest in the world: DM3.60 is charged on 1 kg. green coffee equivalent in addition to VAT; that is, it progressively increases on processed products because of the higher volume of the input of raw material. On the other hand, the tax is comparatively less on expensive qualities than on cheap ones, resulting in the traditionally high quality of West German imports.

Traditionally, Colombia is West Germany's most important supplier with an average of 30 per cent. Brazil follows with a share of between 5 per cent (1979) and 19.2 per cent (1985), followed by Kenya with 5–8 per cent and El Salvador with a share decreasing from nearly 14 per cent (1981) to 5.6 per cent (1986).[7]

The quality of West German imports is actually declining because of the concentration of the industry and the utilisation of advanced mass-production equipment. With the exception of 1986, the year of the Brazilian drought, the demand for mild coffees, the highest quality, has slowly decreased in favour of 'Other Arabicas' from Brazil and Ethiopia, mainly used for filling up the blends of roasters, and in favour of 'Robusta' qualities, used in the production of soluble coffee. In addition to Colombia, this shift mainly reduces imports from Central America, which supplies most of the 'Other Milds' apart from Mexico and Papua–New Guinea (see Table 3.1). The other peculiarity is the extremely low price and income elasticity of demand in the German coffee market. The DIVO Institute[8] calculated a regular elasticity to price change in 1986 of 0.26 in a situation of low price levels and, increasing to 0.41 with higher price levels. In households with a low disposable income it was 0.5; higher up the income scale it decreased to 0.1, independent of prices. These figures

Table 3.1:   West German coffee imports in ICO quality groups[9]
(1980–86; in %)

	1980	1981	1982	1983	1984	1985	1986
Colombian Milds	45.3	43.9	44.2	43.4	42.6	38.8	44.8
Other Milds	30.4	28.9	21.2	20.5	16.6	16.8	18.5
Other Arabicas	9.9	12.4	18.0	19.1	21.1	22.6	11.0
Arabicas[a]	2.2	1.7	3.1	4.6	7.3	8.1	7.3
Robustas	9.7	9.2	9.9	9.0	10.2	11.5	14.8

SOURCE: *DKV Jahresberichte* (Hamburg: Deutschen Kaffee-Verband e.v.) various years; ICO, *Quarterly Statistical Bulletin on Coffee* (London: ICO) various numbers.

NOTE: [a] From ICO exporting countries without basic quota, mainly semi-washed.

reveal the enormous preference of German consumers for coffee and their unwillingness to change their consumption habits, despite price increases. As a consequence of this behaviour the competition within the processing industry did not affect prices until 1984. In spite of a sharp fight for market shares, the industry could be sure of high profit margins.

2.2   The Industrial Structure

Initially coffee was imported to West Germany by a number of small specialist companies. They took care of the import and transport formalities for the small regional roasting companies and supplied them with the qualities they needed for their blends. This structure largely broke down after the removal by law of the import monopoly of these specialists, increasing concentration among coffee processors and their transition into buying and importing for themselves.

The concentration index of UNCTAD, that is, the market share of the four biggest companies, has increased from 49 per cent in 1960 to 67 per cent in 1978.[10] The number of members in the German Coffee Association (roasting and soluble-coffee companies) decreased between 1960 and 1986 from 650 to 76.[11]

B. Rothfos AG, originally belonging to a branch of importers, is the biggest company in the German market in terms of volume of traded coffee. Internationally it ranks second behind General Foods. Today it is vertically diversified over the whole market, from offices in the producing countries to its own processing firms and retail shops. Its main business is import and export trade, the supply of roasters with raw material and the supply of non-branded roasted and soluble coffee, which the customers distribute under their own names. By supply and client processing (for example, Aldi and Eduscho) it controls approximately 27 per cent of the West German market and ranks second among the German soluble-coffee producers. On a world scale the company accounts for about 10 per cent (6.5 million bags) of market production. With only 119 employees, it achieved a turnover in 1985 of DM3.3 billion, double that of 1980.

Only firms with trade marks are visible to the consumer. The market is divided into different kinds of distribution. The 'branchers' distribute the roasted, still unground coffee to branches or deposits in bakeries. It is either ground in the shop or at home. The packagers distribute their brands, which are mostly ground, through retail shops or supermarkets. The largest supermarkets, mainly Aldi, sometimes roast to order to sell their own roasts under their own brand-name or no-name brands.

In 1984 the invention of high-yield roasting technology resulted in a big marketing flop and brought some movement into the distribution of market shares. Simultaneously, this technology reduced the input of raw material and raised the volume of the roasted beans. With a high advertising budget[12] and by claiming the result was a more substantial brew, Tchibo and Jacobs introduced new packages of the same volume but with reduced weight and about DM1 cheaper. In fact, however, this loss of weight meant a price increase of approximately 14 per cent.[13] The consumers saw through this strategy and turned to the suppliers with the old packages. The new packages quickly disappeared from the shelves. This resulted in a fierce battle for the redistribution of market shares which now also affected price policy. At least windfall profits, which often go along with the adaptation of retail prices to new input prices caused by changes in world market prices or rates of exchange were prevented.

In a situation of nearly stagnant market volume and growing importance of supermarkets at the expense of both traditional retailers and the special coffee shops, the different kinds of distribution have also been affected. The branchers begin to build up so-called 'fresh islands', their own sales areas within supermarkets, to distribute coffee and sweets. The packagers use ways of direct distribution through 'shops within a shop' (Jacobs). At the same time the supermarkets increasingly try to make use of the high preference for

Table 3.2: Market shares of the most important brands in West Germany

	Market share 1986 (%)	1982 (%)	Type of distribution	Other activities	Total turnover[a] (DM billions)	Balance surplus (DM millions)	Employees
Tchibo	21	24	B	Cosmetics, beer, cigarettes, non-food sales	2.3[b]	51.7	3822
Jacobs	21	24	P	Chocolate, sweets, banks, export, multinational	2.7[c] (coffee 2.1)	n.a.	2650
Aldi	17	13	D	Groceries	n.a.	n.a.	n.a.
Eduscho[d]	16	15	B	Non-food sales	2[c]	n.a.	3800
HAG–GF[e]	5	7	P	Soft drinks, foodstuff, export	1.1[c]	65[c]	739

SOURCES: *G+J–Forschungsgemeinschaft für Marketing (1987); Tchibo-Geschäftsbericht*, 1986 (Hamburg: Tchibo); *Die Welt*, vol. 13(3) 1987; *Eduscho Pressemitteilung*, vol. 2(3) 1986 (Bremen); *Handbuch der deutschen Aktiengesellschaften, 1986/87* (Darmstadt) p. 27.

NOTES: [a] all activities, German branch; [b] 1986; [c] 1985; [d] 15% held by Rothfos AG; [e] held by Philip Morris via General Foods.
B = brancher; D = discounter; P = packager; n.a. = not available.

coffee. They try to get the customers with attractive special offers for their brand or that of the packagers, sometimes below their own cost price.

The brands listed in Table 3.2 are followed by Melitta with a 4 per cent market share and a total turnover in West Germany of DM1.3 billion (25 per cent coffee) and Dallmayr (50 per cent Nestlé subsidiary) with a 3 per cent market share and DM170 million total turnover of coffee in West Germany. Apart from these seven market leaders, there remains a market share of 13 per cent that is divided among some regionally based roasters or roasters contracted by large supermarkets, and a number of small, so-called 'wash-room roasters' (small regional handicraft roasters).

Concentration in the industry for solubles is even higher than in the field of roasted coffee. This sector, which includes a constant share of 10 per cent of the market, is dominated by the TNC, Nestlé (30 per cent own brands, 20 per cent client production for Aldi).[14] The rest of this market is mainly divided among Jacobs, General Foods

(Maxwell) and the Rothfos subsidiary DEK with no-name client production. The concentration index of UNCTAD increased from the high level of 82 per cent (1968–9) to 94 per cent (1977–8) market share for the four largest firms.

The rising concentration in trade, processing and distribution constitutes a serious obstacle for the purchasing position of the producing countries, especially the smaller ones like those of Central America. The trade volume of only one company, for example Rothfos or Jacobs, exceeds the total trade volume of every Central American country. Such trade volume gives the companies better possibilities to influence stock exchanges through their large demand volumes and long-term contracts. By taking advantage of competition between the producing countries they can force them to accept price discounts in 'special deals'.

2.3   The Distribution of Profits in the Coffee Deal

There are two problems to be found in the various attempts to break down the economic shares of each participant in the coffee trade. The first one is that excess profits are not separated from production costs. The second problem arises from the fact that the composition of export prices in producing countries is analysed at a given level of prices in the world market, or the composition of retail prices is analysed at given import prices in consumer countries. This approach does not take into account the crucial factor in world market prices: the division of profits from the coffee trade between producer and consumer countries.

A calculation based on a precise distinction between profits and production costs is made almost impossible by the practice of blending coffee from different origins. This blending of qualities also mixes different margins of costs and profits into a single product and price. Another problem is the availability and methods of ascertaining statistical data. For example, ground rents and land prices are calculated as production costs, while price discounts and subsidies are rarely listed. I tried to overcome this problem of world market prices in my study *Profit-Bohnen.*[15] It was only satisfactory for the year 1972 because of the problems of availability of data. But even apart from the general restriction of the quality of available data, some reservations have to be made. Production costs had to be partly estimated. The share of land prices and profits from technological advance, economies of scale, speculation, windfall profits from holding stocks and exchange rates, and the utilisation of tax subsidies and tariff preferences could not be assigned to the excess profits. They are still included in the production costs. Production costs in relation to profits tend to be exaggerated because the more expensive alternative was used whenever varying figures were found. As a result, shifts in the distribution of excess profits among the participants are possible as far as these profits don't rise in the same proportion as the calculated distribution.

Discounts, subventions of guaranteed planters' prices and the profits of private export processors (hulling and grading), as far as this is not done by official or semi-official export organisations, could not be apportioned. This means that the profits of the private exporters or export processors are still a part of the ground rent of the producing state. The use of a constant or proportional estimation of transport costs and some processing costs for different qualities and so on may also lead to small inaccuracies.

The estimations have been done for the three principal suppliers of West Germany in 1972: Colombia, Brazil and El Salvador, in relation to their market shares at that time. The uniform retail price in relation to the valuation of the various qualities was differentiated in order to get varying quality-compensated consumer prices.

Bearing in mind the reservations stated above, this calculation of the breakdown of West German retail prices justifies some conclusions. Because of higher production costs the remaining excess profits in El Salvador are relatively low. In 1972 El Salvador was, in relation to the yield per hectare, input costs, wages and so on, the least profitable producer. These figures are valid, with reservations, for Central America too. However, the cost situation in Brazil and Colombia, in contrast to their very different average farm size, manpower input and product quality, was comparable. (See Figure 3.1.)

In none of the countries was the total of all production, trade, transport, processing and distribution costs as high as the retail price paid by the consumers. In all cases the total of all appropriated surplus profits exceeded the total of the production costs. In 1972 world market and retail prices were relatively low. Corresponding estimations for other years show that the share of the production costs in the consumer price, as well as the significance of different production costs, decrease with an increasing level of prices.

With predominantly small and middle-sized high-quality production, the planters in Colombia hold the strongest position against the state. Only here can the planters appropriate a larger share than

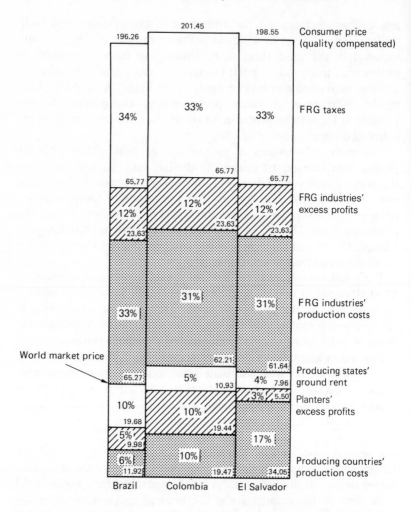

Figure 3.1 *The coffee deal (1972): distribution of costs and profits within the consumer price of German coffee imports from the main suppliers in relation to their market shares (quotations in UScent/lb. green coffee equivalent)*

Market share, 1972: Brazil 8.9%; Colombia 21.78%; El Salvador 13.01%

SOURCE: E. Meister (1986), *Profit-Bohnen* (Mettingen: Brasilienkunde Verlag) p. 181.

NOTE: Production costs include normal (average) profit rate.

the state of the excess profits remaining in the country. At the given level of prices, the excess profits remaining in the producing country amount to only a quarter of total excess profits. The main part remains in the consuming country, West Germany, where it is mainly appropriated by the government. Comparative calculations show that, corresponding to the decreasing significance of production costs, this distribution of excess profits shifts to the benefit of the producing countries as prices rise, for example by production reductions caused by Brazilian frosts. These shifts reduce West Germany's share (absolute profits are higher, of course) to the detriment equally of the state and of industry. The opposite happens in a situation in which production increases faster than demand.

This distribution of excess profits shows that the producing countries are not able to take advantage of their monopolistic position as producers and of the high preference of the consumers. This is due to the high level of competition between them because of the lack of profitable alternatives in agriculture and their weak position on the world market. Every attempt to increase the developing countries' export earnings via higher price levels will fail unless it is caused by a stronger production and selling position, and it has to be taken into account that the main share of those profits will remain within the industrialised countries.

The distribution of the economic surplus between producing and consuming countries is regulated by the export prices of raw materials. Roughly, this distribution relates to the share of production costs, that is, to the value-added share of the final product. Enhancement of the profit share of the producing countries by an increase of export prices would be threatened by a resulting stimulus to increase production. The only stable possibility for such an outcome, apart from a worldwide and effective planning and distribution of limited production and the resulting benefits, is an increase in the degree of processing of the export product.

3. CENTRAL AMERICAN COFFEE IN EUROPE

3.1 The Structure of Trade

In the 1960s the dependence of Central American exports on coffee was very high (1960: Costa Rica 53.9 per cent, El Salvador 65.7 per cent, Guatemala 67.5 per cent, Honduras 18.5 per cent, Nicaragua

Table 3.3:   West Germany 'Other Milds' imports by origin (according to ICO country classification;[a] % of West Germany's total imports)

	1979	1980	1981	1982	1983	1984	1985	1986
El Salvador	13.2	12.1	14.0	9.1	10.5	7.7	6.1	5.6
Ruanda[b]	2.0	1.0	0.9	1.1	1.6	4.4	4.7	4.0
Papua-New Guinea	4.3	4.9	2.5	2.1	2.6	2.3	3.5	3.7
Burundi[b]	0.9	1.2	0.9	2.0	3.0	3.1	3.4	3.3
Costa Rica	3.2	2.9	3.4	3.2	2.1	2.1	1.9	2.3
Guatemala	6.0	4.5	4.1	3.0	2.0	1.4	1.8	2.1
Mexico	1.9	1.7	0.9	0.7	0.6	0.6	0.5	1.6
Nicaragua	3.7	2.3	2.0	1.9	1.9	1.3	1.4	1.0
Honduras	2.7	2.1	1.6	1.3	0.8	0.5	0.9	0.6
Ecuador	1.4	0.6	n.a.	n.a.	n.a.	n.a.	0.3	0.6
Peru	n.a.	n.a.	n.a.	n.a.	n.a.	n.a.	0.03	0.6
India	0.5	0.2	n.a.	n.a.	0.7	0.7	0.4	0.6

SOURCE: *DKV-Jahresberichte*, various years.

NOTES: [a] Without 'all others'; [b] 'Arabicas' without basic quota (mainly 'semi-washed'); n.a. = not available.

30.7 per cent).[16] While the figures remained on a high level in the 1980s (see Table 2.6 of the preceding chapter in this volume), there seemed to be a faster growing importance of coffee exports in relation to the total exports in most African producing countries. This not only indicates a certain tendency to export diversification in Central America, it also corresponds to the cost advantage of 'Robusta' production and the relatively quick rise of African 'Robusta' and 'Colombian Milds' exports in relation to the (mainly Central American) quality group of the 'Other Milds' in the world market.

Corresponding to the West German imports in the quality groups shown in Table 3.1 'Other Milds' West German imports are shown in Table 3.3. The development of the supply shares and the suggested relative decrease of 'Other Milds' imports can be seen, irrespective of the absolute supply volume. In 1979 the share of total imports was 39.58 per cent and even though the drought in Brazil in 1986 was compensated by 'Other Milds' also, the share fell to 25.87 per cent (1985: 24.88 per cent).

Furthermore, the recent quality loss of West Germany's imports hurt the Central American producers almost exclusively (with some impact on the Mexican and Ecuadorians also). The share of the Central American countries fell from 28.76 per cent in 1979 to 11.52

per cent in 1986 while other suppliers of this quality were able to increase their share from 10.82 per cent to 14.35 per cent in the same period. The African suppliers of this quality, Ruanda and Burundi, and Papua–New Guinea in the Pacific had a special advantage.

A comparison with the structure of supply in other quality groups shows that only with 'Robustas' is there the same diversified structure of suppliers and the same equal distribution of market shares. This structure not only increases the competition between suppliers but also decreases their selling position. This intensified during the 1980s and contrasts very strongly with the structure of suppliers in the groups of 'Colombian Milds' and 'Other Arabicas'.

3.2 The Accusation of Discrimination by EEC–ACP Tariff Preferences

Loss of market share, compared to the increase by other suppliers, led the most affected Central American countries to make the accusation of discrimination by the tariff preferences of the EEC in favour of members of the Lomé Agreement. GATT has called for an end to this distortion of competition by a suspension of the EEC's external tariffs on green coffee also. Coffee plays the most important part in this agreement, with 40 per cent of the trade volume of all agricultural raw materials in it.[17] But none of the important South and Central American producers belong to the group of associated countries. On the other hand, all African and Pacific producers are represented, with the exception of Angola.

The EEC maintained internal taxes and in 1964 guaranteed duty-free imports for a number of raw materials to the members of the Jaunde Agreement. In the following years this preference was widened to the members of the Arusha Agreement (1971) and the ensuing Lomé Agreement (1975).

Apart from the above-mentioned internal coffee tax, an import tariff of DM1/kg. on green coffee was effective in West Germany before 1964. However, this alone corresponds to approximately 25 per cent of the value. On 1 July 1964 this tariff was reduced to 12 per cent for the non-associated countries and was again reduced on 1 July 1968 to the EEC common tariff of 9.6 per cent. Since 1 July 1971 the EEC's General System of Preferences was effective with a tariff of 7 per cent for all developing countries. All non-associated coffee producing countries exporting to the EEC were affected by this. Temporarily in November 1976, and finally at the Tokyo Round, the tariff was generally reduced to 7 per cent and again on 1 January 1987 to 4.5 per cent. Apart from this, a duty-free import share exists for least-developed countries, but as far as coffee is concerned this affects only Haiti (1 per cent of EEC's coffee imports) which is the only non-ACP member as well as the 'least-developed' coffee exporter.

In the case of processed coffee a duty-free import share for least-developed and ACP countries is also effective. Since the Tokyo Round, exporters from developing countries (GSP) are charged a tariff of 9 per cent for green coffee, 12 per cent for roasted coffee not freed of caffeine, 18 per cent for decaffeinated and 9 per cent for soluble coffee and extracts. In addition, an import quota of 19,100 tons (West Germany tranch 1,712t.) exists for soluble coffee.[18]

The accusation of discrimination seems to be justified by these rates of tariffs and the shift of exports, for example in West Germany. But in the case of processed coffee, discrimination in practice is more or less out of question. With the exception of the Ivory Coast and Tanzania, none of the ACP countries has an export capacity comparable to that of Latin America. Here the different rates of industrialisation have stronger effects than tariff differences, even though these are higher in the case of processed products. But the Central American exports, for example of soluble coffee, are also very low. In the case of tariffs on processed coffee it seems to be more relevant to analyse trade prevention than trade discrimination.[19]

In the case of green coffee, the reduction of GSP tariffs diminishes the degree of preferences strongly. So the Institute for World Economy in Kiel, in a study requested by the West German government, argues that these tariffs have only minor effects upon retail prices and do not affect the volume of demand. Because of this they come to the conclusion that there is no discrimination.[20] However, this argument only refers to the influence of tariffs on the total import volume, but not to shifts in the origins of imports within a given volume; that is, it refers to trade reduction but not to trade diversion. With given qualities and retail prices, an importer who tries to reduce cost prices of course makes use of small cost differences. Small tariff differences can play an important role in his purchase decision although they do not influence retail prices (see Table 3.4).

On the other hand, differences in production costs, national export prices, granted discounts, differences in transport costs and fluctuations of the price differences among the quality groups have a relatively stronger influence on cost prices than the existing rate of tariff differences. But because the tariffs are charged on the value of

Table 3.4: Fluctuation of the price relation between 'Other Milds' and 'Robustas' (price differential of 'Robustas' as % of 'Other Milds' price)

1976–7	1977–8	1978–9	1979–80	1980–1	1981–2	1982–3	1983–4	1984–5
3.56	11.55	1.56	7.35	12.99	25.59	6.66	5.44	14.64

SOURCE: *The Economist* Intelligence Unit (1987), *Coffee to 1991* (London: *The Economist*) p. 54.

imports, the effect of tariff differences grows in relation to the level of quality and prices. Because of this, the share of EEC imports from ACP countries grows in periods of rising prices while it falls with decreasing prices (see Table 3.5).

From these facts it can be concluded that tariff discrimination in the form of trade diversion has a declining influence, depending on the level of prices and the price differential of qualities. More important for trade diversion are aspects like quality shifts in the demand of the processing industry and changes in the relative price differential between the quality groups, granted discounts and the competition between producers. However, because Central America suffers from these factors too and exports a relative high quality, an additional disadvantage is arising from the tariff preferences.

More important for the EEC scheme and the ACP countries, but with only a small influence, if any, on the shifts of the EEC's import structure, are the financial transfers from the STABEX fund. As they have no direct influence on export prices, however, they are without significance for the purchase decision of the private importer or roaster. In the case of coffee these transfers amounted to a total of 186.2 million ECUs (1975–84).[21]

4. CONCLUSIONS

The coffee market in the EEC is the most important coffee market in the world. Nevertheless the relative share of Central American coffee in this market is declining. The main customers of most of these countries, with the exception of El Salvador, are the USA and Canada. Central American coffee exports suffer from various factors.

The producer countries in general, and Central America in particular, have only a small share in the distribution of economic surplus from the coffee trade, due to overproduction, the lack of

Table 3.5:   The impact of price level on the coffee exports of selected ACP countries to the EEC (prices in US cents/lb.; share of exports to the EEC from total coffee exports in %)

	1977	1978	1979	1980	1981	1982	1983
Share of EEC exports							
Kenya (Col. Milds)	66.64	69.03	77.75	73.86	67.63	60.47	66.85
Ivory Coast (Robustas)	61.53	58.10	64.37	n.a.	57.17	58.37	65.84
Cameroon (Robustas)	80.85	83.68	82.94	82.27	n.a.	73.26	n.a.
Tanzania (Col. Milds)	60.48	59.15	68.90	65.39	63.96	n.a.	n.a.
Ethiopia (Other Arabicas)	n.a.	n.a.	22.21	31.07	30.98	34.94	n.a.
ICO composite indicator price (annual average)	229.21	155.16	169.50	150.67	115.48	125.46	127.70

SOURCE: Own calculations from Eurostat (1986), *Foreign Trade, Third Countries: Statistical Yearbook, 1977–1983*, 6C, vol. A (Luxemburg: European Community); *The Economist* Intelligence Unit (1987), *Coffee to 1991* (London: *The Economist*) p. 54.

NOTE: n.a. = not available.

export alternatives and their weak trading position. Increased income from the export of coffee, for example by an increase in the degree of value-adding processing and a lowering of input costs, is prevented by the oligopolistic concentration of the industry in the EEC, the sharp competition for market share, the level of necessary investment for the introduction of new brands as well as by tariff barriers and import quotas. With its higher level of processing capacity, this is more an obstacle to Central American exports than to those from Africa.

The quality group 'Other Milds', which is mainly produced in Central America, is subject to the substitutional competition of the higher quality 'Colombian Milds' as well as of the cheaper 'Other Arabicas'. Shifts in the structure of demand impede the exports of this quality group. Although of minor importance, discrimination by tariff preferences also affects Central American green coffee exports. It should be considered whether, among other possibilities, forms of direct marketing (labelled as brand of origin) are appropriate schemes to improve the difficult position of Central American coffee.

Notes

1. 1984; in three-digit SITC groups; UN (1986), *International Trade Statistics Yearbook, 1984*, vol. 2 (New York: United Nations).
2. Calculated in values in US$ from UN, op. cit.
3. DKV (Deutscher Kaffee Verband) (1984), *Jahresbericht 1984* (Hamburg: DKV); in 1986 nearly 10 million bags were imported; re-exports included in both cases.
4. Green coffee equivalent = roasted coffee × 1.9, or extracts × 3; all figures from DKV, *Jahresbericht 1986* (Hamburg: DKV).
5. Leopoldo Pineda-Serna (1980), *Las Exportaciones Latinoamericanas de Café hacia la Comunidad Economica Europea. Pasado, Presente y Futuro*, Documentos de trabajo no. 28 (Gotinga: Instituto Iberoamericano de Investigaciones Economicas, Universidad de Gotinga) p. 27f.
6. DKV, *Jahresbericht 1986*, op. cit.; *The Economist* Intelligence Unit (1987), *Coffee to 1991: Controlling a Surplus* (London: *The Economist*) p. 46.
7. DKV, *Jahresbericht*, op. cit., various years.
8. DIVO Institut (1968), 'Der Bohnenkaffeemarkt in der Bundesrepublik', in *DIVO Informationen*, Reihe 1 (March) pp. 6ff.
9. Calculated from ICO quality assignment to countries; but some countries produce smaller amounts of other qualities too; without consideration of 'all other countries' in the import statistics.
10. UNCTAD (1984), *Studies in Processing, Marketing and Distribution of Commodities: The Processing and Marketing of Coffee* (New York: UNCTAD Secretariat) p. 21.
11. DKV, *Jahresberichte*, op. cit., various years.
12. The advertising budget for coffee, tea and cocoa reaches rank 8 of all industries; for coffee alone it amounted in 1986 to DM213 million.
13. Axel Springer Verlag (1984), *Märkte: Informationen für die Werbeplanung – Kaffee, Tee, Kakao* (Berlin: Marketing Anzeigen) p. 29.
14. Ibid., p. 36.
15. Elmar Meister (1986), *Profit-Bohnen* (Mettingen: Brasilienkunde Verlag) p. 174ff.
16. Peter J. Buzzanell (1979), *Coffee Production and Trade in Latin America* (Washington, D.C.: US Dept. of Agriculture, Foreign Agricultural Service).
17. Of the 65 countries, who have signed the Lomé III Agreement, 35 were coffee exporters, 26 members of the ICO. Of these the following were regularly exporting more than 10,000 tonnes: Burundi, Cameroon, Central African Republic, Ethiopia, Ivory Coast, Kenya, Papua–New Guinea, Ruanda, Tanzania, Uganda and Zaire.
18. UNCTAD (1984) op. cit., p. 40; Axel Borrmann *et al.* (1979), *The Significance of EEC's Generalized System of Preferences* (Tübingen: HWWA-Inst. für Weltwirtschaft, Univ. Kiel).
19. In this sense the German Coffee Association (DKV) supports the suspension of tariffs on green coffee, but defends tariffs in the case of processed forms. *Mitteilungen des DKV*, Rundschreiben 24/86, 3 Dec. 1986.

20. Jamuna P. Agarwal *et al.* (1985), *EC Trade Policies Towards Associated Developing Countries: Barriers to Success* (Tübingen: Inst. für Weltwirtschaft, Univ. Kiel) and subsequent studies from this Institute.
21. Eurostat (1986), *ACP Basic Statistics, 1986* (Luxemburg: European Community).

4 Export Agriculture and Crisis in Central America: Labour Market Problems in Nicaragua

Jan P. de Groot and Harrie Clemens

1. INTRODUCTION

Colonial policies of a feudal and mercantilistic character laid the foundations for a dual economic system in Central America, in which commercial agriculture was associated with production for export and subsistence agriculture with food production. Export agriculture was concentrated in the *haciendas*, which exacted cheap labour from the indigenous sector. After independence and the collapse of the Central American Republic in 1839, the five small nations embraced economic liberalism as a guiding doctrine. Liberalism contained a new political model for the post-colonial state as well as an economic programme. Free trade and specialisation according to comparative advantage were seen as dynamic forces of economic development. Public policies were redirected and resources reallocated to the development of new agricultural commodities for export, in particular coffee and bananas. Thus the colonial economy was transformed into a larger and more productive one, but its dual character was maintained (Quirós, 1971:33, 93). Although vulnerable to world market conditions, the Central American economies expanded rapidly until the economic crisis of 1973. After the Second World War there was a new round of expansion of export agriculture.

Central America's rapid economic growth in the 1960s was supported by export earnings which increased 10 per cent a year on average (Williams 1986:4). Regional coffee and banana exports almost doubled, but non-traditional exports increased still faster; cotton and beef became the two most important new exports. These exports provided foreign exchange for the import of modern agricultural technologies and encouraged investment by multinational

71

corporations, local farmers and businessmen. Modernisation brought prosperity to these groups, but at the same time a large number of peasants were evicted from the land. As in the past, export-led growth caused serious social distortions (Torres-Rivas, 1980:25).

The Central American crisis and social and political unrest in the region to a large degree reflect the intensification of the struggle over land and over the means of survival. The peasantry does not accept dispossession from the land, its basic means of subsistence. The export boom of the 1960s and 1970s brought rapid economic growth and export diversification. As in the past, the economies grew and became more productive as the region was further integrated into the world economic system. But the living conditions of large numbers of peasants, who lost access to land and came to depend on seasonal and insecure work, deteriorated.

Nicaragua essentially followed the same Central American agro-export model but it differed in some respects. The country was late in developing its export agriculture and the participation of small and medium-size producers was higher than elsewhere in the region. After the 1979 revolution, the Sandinista regime tried to maintain a high level of exports. One of the problems it encountered was a labour shortage in export crops. In the discussion of this labour problem an important element is the perception of the structural characteristics of the agro-export sector. This is a crucial issue for agricultural policy as it refers to the role of the peasants in export agriculture and their access to land. In this chapter the main points of view of this debate are summed up. An analysis of recent and earlier survey data is used to show that, for the case of coffee, the conflicting perceptions can partly be reduced to regional differences. After outlining these regional variations in coffee production systems and its related class relations, labour problems in the coffee sector are discussed and tentative conclusions formulated.

2. NICARAGUA'S AGRO-EXPORT SECTOR

Nicaragua, compared with the other Central American countries, was late in developing its export agriculture. As a consequence, the export activities that developed more recently, such as cotton and beef, became relatively more important in Nicaragua than the traditional sectors. Also, as a result of this late development and a lower population density, the structure of the Nicaraguan agro-export sector differs substantially from that of other Central American countries, in the sense that in Nicaragua there is a higher participation of small and medium-size producers in agro-export activities (see Section 3). Before the Second World War the country's export economy did not reach a degree of development comparable with that of Costa Rica, Guatemala or El Salvador. Coffee was the main commercial crop and provided the earliest basis for capital accumulation. But ecological limitations in the Pacífico Central and insufficient development of the transport system in the interior prevented further expansion of the crop. Production increased from a yearly average of 9,700 tons in the period 1909–18 to 14,300 in 1929–38 (Quirós, 1971:66). Bananas formed the next important agro-export activity. But the country failed to develop an important banana industry, not so much because of a lack of appropriate ecological conditions, in particular on the Atlantic Coast, but rather as a consequence of conflicts with the banana companies over navigational rights. In 1911 exports amounted to 83,200 tons, this volume fell to 45,000 tons annually in the period just before the Second World War and to 7,500 tons in the postwar years 1945–9 (ibid., 76).

In the 1950s the agro-export sector expanded rapidly. Cultivation of coffee and bananas increased, but cotton production contributed most to this accelerated growth. In the 1960s there was a further expansion and diversification of the agro-export economy as exports of beef, sugar, sesame and tobacco developed. Foreign exchange surpluses gained during the Second World War were used for public investments in rural infrastructure, energy and ports. This, together with the insecticide revolution constituted the basis for expansion of cotton cultivation in the Pacific plain. Due to the fluctuation of prices on the world market this expansion had a cyclical course. The area increased from 14,000 hectares in 1950 to 84,000 in 1954. New peaks were subsequently reached in 1966 and 1974 and in 1978 the area had grown to 212,000 hectares, which included a considerable part of land of marginal quality.

The cotton acreage expanded at the expense of the area in basic grain production. Before cotton came to the Pacific plain peasants had access to the land of livestock *haciendas* as sharecroppers or as workers who had obtained the usufruct of a subsistence plot. The peasants as well as the *haciendas* combined livestock activities with the production of basic grains. When cotton cultivation expanded, the peasants had to pay money rents for the land they used, which they only were able to do if they engaged in cotton cultivation on a modest scale. Some of them did so, but many peasants lost access to the land, and the acreage in basic grains decreased almost proportionally to the expansion of the cotton area. Between 1952 and 1966, for example, the acreage under cotton in the three main producing departments of this crop, Chinandega, León and Managua, increased from 10,000 to 43,000 hectares, whereas simultaneously the area under basic grains and sesame decreased by the same amount from 55,000 to 22,000 hectares (Quirós, ibid., 185).

From the late 1950s cotton had surpassed coffee as a foreign-exchange earner, but also in terms of rural employment. The area under coffee meanwhile expanded from 56,000 hectares in 1950 to 86,000 hectares in 1976. Over that same period yields almost doubled, increasing from 330 kg. per hectare to over 600. Part of the coffee cultivation was modernised, but most was produced by traditional methods. When compared with coffee production in neighbouring countries productivity in Nicaragua is low.

In the 1960s beef exports developed rapidly as the export possibilities to US markets expanded. An increasing demand for low-cost industrial meat in the US coincided with rising costs of US producers and with decreasing Argentine exports. Nicaragua's beef exports increased from 10 million lb. in 1960 to 54 million in 1970 and 58 million in 1976. In 1960 cotton, coffee and beef exports together accounted for 65 per cent of the value of all exports; in 1977 this figure was almost 60 per cent, while other agricultural exports represented 9 per cent of total value (see Table 4.1).

As indicated, in the 1970s the export boom continued, in particular the area under cotton still expanded substantially, that of other export crops augmented only slightly. The cotton area that reached a peak of 150,000 hectares in 1965–6 was cut back to 95,400 hectares in 1970–1, and subsequently increased again to 212,400 hectares in 1977–8, a record level not surpassed since.

In 1970 agricultural exports amounted to US $111 million; they increased to US $177 million in 1973, then doubled in 1976 to US $354 million and reached unprecedented levels in 1977 and 1978 when the value increased to US $425 and US $446 million respectively (see Table 4.1). In 1977 and 1978 international coffee prices were very high, coffee producers picked all they could. Cotton and beef prices were good. Livestock producers concerned by the political developments in the country slaughtered more animals than ever before. They converted their stock into flight-capital or moved their cattle over the borders to Costa Rica or Honduras. There was a

Table 4.1: Nicaragua: agricultural exports, 1970–86 (US $'000,000)

	1970	1971	1972	1973	1974	1975	1976	1977	1978	1979	1980	1981	1982	1983	1984	1985	1986
Crop exports	84.4	91.0	124.1	132.4	207.2	199.2	317.1	388.1	378.0	331.6	235.7	344.5	268.8	325.2	299.1	245.4	—
Cotton	34.2	41.3	62.9	63.2	135.9	95.6	130.6	150.6	140.9	135.7	30.4	123.4	87.2	109.5	133.8	91.0	—
Coffee	32.1	29.3	33.0	44.4	46.1	48.1	119.4	198.8	199.6	158.5	165.7	136.8	124.0	153.7	122.4	122.6	—
Sugar	9.8	11.6	15.2	13.5	12.3	42.6	52.8	27.8	19.6	19.6	20.5	51.0	36.4	34.4	20.9	7.4	—
Bananas	0.3	..	3.4	5.6	5.3	4.9	4.6	4.5	4.8	6.4	8.4	20.9	9.8	14.8	11.9	14.9	—
Sesame	2.3	2.0	1.6	0.7	0.8	1.6	1.2	1.8	3.4	3.2	6.3	5.1	5.8	5.8	5.9	5.5	—
Tobacco	1.9	2.3	3.6	2.9	3.9	2.9	4.7	4.5	3.0	3.0	1.4	3.7	4.4	3.5	4.2	4.0	—
Other	3.8	4.5	4.4	2.1	2.9	3.5	3.8	0.1	6.7	5.2	3.0	3.6	1.2	3.5	–	–	—
Beef	26.6	28.7	38.3	44.5	21.9	27.0	37.6	37.3	67.7	93.5	58.6	23.2	33.8	31.4	17.6	12.0	—
Total agric. exports	111.0	119.7	162.4	176.9	229.1	226.2	354.7	425.4	445.7	425.1	294.3	367.7	302.6	356.6	316.7	257.4	—
Total exports	176.6	187.2	249.2	277.9	380.9	375.2	549.9	636.8	646.0	566.6	450.4	508.2	405.5	431.8	385.8	301.6	219.0

SOURCE: UNAN (1987a), Table 14 (based on information provided by Banco Central de Nicaragua).

considerable reduction of the national livestock herd. From 1970 to 1978 the value of agro-exports increased continuously. As indicated, the volume of cotton exports expanded, coffee prices climbed to a high level especially at the end of this period and livestock exports increased as a consequence of the political developments in the country (see Table 4.2).

Given the exceptional conditions of 1977 and 1978, it was to be expected that it would be difficult for the Sandinista government to maintain the high levels of export values after 1979. The reconstruction after the revolution, the redistribution of income, the public investment programme of the government and, since 1983, the war with the 'contras', all put pressure on the import demand. In 1980 agricultural exports decreased, mainly because in the 1979–80 cotton season, plantings had been made at the appropriate time on only 20 per cent of the area sown the year before. Total export of goods in that year covered only half of the value of imports. And this situation worsened over time. In 1986 exports covered only one quarter of imports (SPP, 1987:156). The Sandinista regime has not been very successful in recovering and maintaining equilibrium in the trade balance. Imports almost doubled compared with pre-revolutionary levels, and although agricultural exports soon recovered to the level reached in the early 1970s their growth was insufficient to stop the increasing gap.

Cotton production has recovered the least (see Table 4.3). After the unsuccessful harvest of 1979–80 the area planted increased gradually and in 1983–4 reached 60 per cent of the high pre-revolutionary level. Since then production has been decreasing. Low international prices, the high foreign exchange input requirements and labour scarcity are the main factors to explain this reduction. Cotton is an annual crop and producers can easily switch to other activities (Colburn, 1986:51). The government thus provided stronger incentives for this crop than for a permanent crop such as coffee, where investment is more of a fixed nature. But the response of large capitalist enterprises in particular to these incentives has been low. Other classes of cotton producers have encountered serious agronomic, ecological and economic problems. Now, because of the low profitability of cotton cultivation, the government aims to concentrate production in areas of optimal conditions. This contraction of the cotton area will not affect the provision of fibres to the national textile industry, and the production of substitutes is foreseen as far as prime materials for the vegetable oil and animal feed industry are concerned (SPP, 1987:47).

Table 4.2: Export volume, price and value, 1970–86

		1970	1971	1972	1973	1974	1975	1976	1977	1978	1979	1980	1981	1982	1983	1984	1985
Cotton[a]	volume ('000 cwt.)	1474	1687	2211	2164	2868	2881	2455	2531	2801	2470	427	1627	1351	1726	1809	1458
	price (US $/cwt.)	23.2	24.5	28.4	29.2	47.4	33.2	53.2	59.5	50.3	54.9	71.2	75.9	64.5	63.5	74.0	62.4
	value (million US $)	34.2	41.3	62.9	63.2	135.9	95.6	130.6	150.6	140.9	135.7	30.4	123.4	87.2	109.5	133.8	91.0
Coffee[b]	volume ('000 cwt.)	650	704	714	811	703	880	1143	1078	1188	1204	1000	1132	1012	1423	892	898
	price (US $/cwt.)	49.4	41.6	46.3	54.7	65.6	54.6	104.4	184.8	168.0	131.6	165.7	120.9	122.5	108.5	137.3	136.5
	value (million US $)	32.1	29.3	33.0	44.4	46.1	48.1	119.4	198.8	199.6	158.5	165.7	136.8	124.0	153.7	122.4	122.6
Sugar[c]	volume ('000 cwt.)	1545	1593	2168	1790	1461	1964	3239	2157	2126	1974	1348	2232	2066	2376	2200	1347
	price (US $/cwt.)	6.4	7.3	7.0	7.6	8.4	21.7	16.3	12.9	9.2	9.9	15.2	22.9	17.6	14.5	9.4	5.5
	value (million US $)	9.8	11.6	15.2	13.5	12.3	42.6	52.8	27.8	19.6	19.6	20.5	51.0	36.4	34.4	20.9	7.4
Bananas	volume ('000 boxes)	258	..	2431	5775	6327	6630	5955	5677	6012	5637	5694	4907	2283	4288	4166	4387
	price (US $/box)	1.0	..	1.4	1.0	0.8	0.7	0.8	0.8	0.8	1.1	1.1	4.3	4.3	3.5	2.9	3.4
	value (million US $)	0.3	..	3.4	5.6	5.3	4.9	4.6	4.5	4.8	6.4	8.4	20.9	9.8	14.8	11.9	14.9
Sesame	volume ('000 cwt.)	128	106	88	38	38	75	56	59	111	106	117	118	108	100	147	125
	price (US $/cwt.)	17.7	18.4	18.4	17.6	20.5	22.1	21.8	29.8	30.7	29.7	53.7	43.6	53.9	58.9	40.2	44.1
	value (million US $)	2.3	2.0	1.6	0.7	0.8	1.6	1.2	1.8	3.4	3.2	6.3	5.1	5.8	5.8	5.9	5.5
Tobacco[d]	value (million US $)	1.9	2.3	3.6	2.9	3.9	2.9	4.7	4.5	3.0	3.0	1.4	3.7	4.4	3.5	4.2	4.0
Beef	volume (million lbs)	53.7	54.8	65.2	57.4	34.7	47.7	57.4	58.1	74.9	78.3	45.1	20.9	32.0	31.3	19.8	13.5
	price (US $/lb.)	0.5	0.5	0.6	0.8	0.6	0.6	0.7	0.6	0.9	1.2	1.3	1.1	1.1	1.0	0.9	0.9
	value (million US $)	26.6	28.7	38.3	44.5	21.9	27.0	37.6	37.3	67.7	93.5	58.6	23.2	33.8	31.4	17.6	12.0

SOURCE: See Table 4.1.

NOTES: [a] Cotton ginned; [b] Coffee milled; [c] Raw sugar; [d] Tobacco leaf.
See also Table 4.3.

Table 4.3: Export crops, area, yield and production, from 1969–70 to 1985–6

	1969–70	1970–1	1971–2	1972–3	1973–4	1974–5	1975–6	1976–7	1977–8	1978–9	1979–80	1980–1	1981–2	1982–3	1983–4	1984–5	1985–6
Cotton area ('000 manzanas)[a]	155.1	136.3	156.1	210.9	259.4	254.4	204.6	283.0	303.4	248.2	54.6	134.6	132.7	129.2	167.6	164.3	123.2
yield (cwt./mz)[b]	9.6	12.6	14.3	10.9	12.2	10.5	11.7	9.0	8.8	9.9	8.7	12.2	10.5	13.6	11.3	10.3	
production ('000 cwt)	1489	1712	2231	2304	3174	2671	2397	2557	2673	2466	474	1646	1387	1757	1881	1700	
Coffee area ('000 manzanas)	124.3	120.1	118.4	118.6	118.9	119.0	120.0	120.0	120.0	135.0	140.0	134.7	128.0	133.5	132.0	131.4	133.5
yield (cwt./mz)[c]	5.9	7.1	7.7	6.4	6.7	7.5	8.9	10.7	10.0	9.4	8.8	9.3	10.4	11.7	8.1	8.2	8.0
production ('000) cwt	737	857	913	763	798	891	1068	1288	1200	1263	1228	1249	1328	1568	1070	1075	1066
Sugar area ('000 manzanas)[d]	42.7	45.8	44.0	43.1	44.6	51.5	58.7	59.6	57.4	59.3	53.1	59.3	64.5	68.0	65.0	64.0	63.8
yield (short tons/mz)	46.2	46.2	43.8	40.5	43.8	44.3	49.5	46.2	47.6	50.3	44.5	45.1	48.3	45.0	43.6	45.8	42.1
production ('000 short tons)	1972	2116	1927	1746	1953	2281	2906	2754	2734	2980	2364	2672	3116	3061	2833	2934	2685
Bananas area ('000 manzanas)	n.a.	0.6	n.a.	3.3	3.3	3.3	3.3	3.3	3.5	3.5	3.6	4.2	3.9	3.8	3.2	3.8	3.8
yield (boxes/mz)[e]	n.a.	1500	n.a.	731	1479	1688	1949	1810	1739	1735	1810	1520	1620	1180	2150	1640	1570
production ('000 boxes)	n.a.	900	n.a.	2412	4881	5570	6432	5973	6087	6074	6523	6386	6309	4479	6895	6249	5951
Sesame area ('000 manzanas)	16.4	14.0	11.0	7.3	6.1	6.5	9.3	8.3	8.6	9.0	25.0	33.0	20.5	13.9	22.0	24.3	
yield (cwt./mz)	9.8	10.4	9.2	10.7	12.2	10.5	9.2	9.1	11.7	14.0	7.3	6.3	7.8	8.0	10.7	6.4	
production ('000 cwt.)	160	146	101	78	74	68	86	76	101	126	182	207	160	111	235	155	
Tobacco area ('000 manzanas)	0.6	0.7	0.7	0.7	0.9	1.0	1.1	0.8	0.9	1.0	0.9	1.3	1.0	1.1	0.9	1.2	
yield (cwt./mz)[f]	26	23	24	24	26	32	30	29	29	29	30	27	24	26	20	23	
production ('000 cwt.)[f]	15.5	16.2	17.0	17.1	23.7	31.5	33.2	23.2	25.9	29.0	27.2	34.9	24.0	28.2	18.3	27.5	

SOURCE: UNAN (1987a), Table 8; and information supplied by MIDINRA.

NOTES:
[a] 1 manzana = 0.7 ha.
[b] Cotton ginned; a cwt. = 46 kg.
[c] Coffee milled.
[d] Sugar cane; a short ton = 2000 Am. lbs = 848.4 kg.
[e] A box of 42.42 kg.
[f] Tobacco leaf.
n.a. = data not available.

Coffee production suffered little from the 1979 revolution and the volume harvested increased even up till 1982–3. The state farms cover 14 per cent of the coffee area of which more than half is under traditional technology. The efficiency of state farms is low, production costs are relatively high. In 1981–2 the government started a coffee renovation scheme on 8,400 hectares, about 10 per cent of the total coffee area. This scheme was over-ambitious and caused a reduction in the coffee harvest at least in the first years of implementation. The incentives for the coffee sector were insufficient to keep producers investing in coffee production. After 1981–2 the overvalued exchange rate reduced the real prices the producers received. And together with labour shortages this has led coffee farmers to reduce the costs of maintaining their plantations even at the expense of a decline in future yields.

Sugar and bananas were seriously hit by the US boycott, but when other market outlets were found, the increase in area and production continued. Beef production recovered only partly from the herd reduction in the period 1978–80, but since 1984 official production figures show a decline. The war situation has had a considerable impact on livestock production, because the humid regions of Chontales and Boaco, the two most important livestock departments, are particularly affected by 'contra' activities. The seasonal migration of cattle from the dry to the rainy zones is hampered by the war. Illegal slaughter seems to have increased, making production figures less reliable. But beef exports have declined partly in response to lower export prices.

3. THE STRUCTURE OF NICARAGUA'S AGRO-EXPORT SECTOR

In the first section it was emphasised that the export-led growth model of the Central American countries gave rise to a dual economic system. In the course of time export agriculture was concentrated in large estates, traditional semi-feudal *haciendas* in the past and modern capitalistic estates in contemporary agro-export development. Every round of agro-export expansion brought loss of land and new forms of subordination to small farmers. Such dualism served to draw cheap labour from the peasantry. In Nicaragua this dualist nature of the agricultural economy is undeniable but less pronounced than in other Central American countries. Probably as a consequence

Table 4.4: Contribution to production of export crops and participation
in livestock numbers by classes of agricultural producers, 1970–1
(percentages)

Classes	Farm size (ha.)	Sugar	Cotton	Tobacco	Coffee	Sesame	Live-stock[a]
Subfamily and family farms	<35	3.4	5.3	46.0	52.1	71.7	21.6
Medium size farmers I	35–140	8.5	17.6	40.6	36.8	8.3	29.0
Medium size farmers II	140–350	9.6	34.7	6.0	8.4	20.0	12.3
Large capitalist estates	>350	78.5	42.4	7.4	2.7	—	37.1

SOURCE: Agricultural Census 1971, as reproduced by Warnken (1975:34, 36).

NOTE: [a] In the livestock sector farm size limits are <70 ha., 70–350 ha., 350–700 ha. and >700 ha.

of a much lower man/land ratio in Nicaragua and of its relatively late development of the agro-export sector, land distribution is less skewed and a class of medium-size farmers has a higher participation in export crop production. This specific class is defined by a farm size between 35 and 350 hectares, those with smaller farms (designated I in Table 4.4) occupy between 35 and 140 hectares, those with larger farms (II) between 140 and 350 hectares. In the livestock sector land-use is more extensive and a farm size twice as large is used to define this class and its subclasses. Medium-size farmers directly participate in farmwork, although they also hire wage labour. They try to maximise profits and thus respond to prices and economic incentives, but because of their dependence on commercial, financial and agro-industrial capital their surplus is often exacted (Kaimowitz, 1986:103). In Table 4.4, based on Warnken's elaboration of the agricultural census of 1971, the contribution to gross production is presented for the different classes in the agrarian sector. With respect to the livestock sector, the figures indicate participation in terms of livestock numbers, as the contribution to production is more difficult to establish.

These data indicate that the contribution of medium-size farmers to exports was substantial. For 1970–1 it can be estimated that the smaller medium-size farmers contributed 24 per cent of the export value of crops, the larger ones participated with 21 per cent and family and subfamily farms with 25 per cent. Together these classes provided about 70 per cent, whereas the agrarian bourgeoisie, the large capitalist estates, contributed 30 per cent of the export value of crops. With respect to the livestock sector, it can be estimated that large capitalist producers had a larger share in beef exports. Smaller livestock farms tend to specialise more in cattle breeding and larger farms in fattening, which is the last stage of the cycle. Small and medium producers provide some of the animals for the large ranches, and these in their turn sell to the export slaughterhouses and meat-packers.

The Sandinista regime has paid much attention to export agriculture; in various ways the agro-export sector received priority in economic policy. But developments in the international economy, the growing military conflict, the US-supported 'contra' war and the political opposition of the agro-export bourgeoisie has made these policies less and less successful. But it has also been stated that the Sandinista policies were hampered by a misconceived perception of the structure of the agro-export sector (Baumeister and Neira, 1986:294–300; Vilas, 1984:107; Kaimowitz, 1986:101).

Kaimowitz states that the Sandinista perception of pre-revolutionary agrarian structure was one of a dualist model with an agrarian bourgeoisie and a semi-proletariat as the two most important classes. In this perception Nicaraguan agriculture was characterised on the one hand by a modern agro-export sector dominated by an agrarian bourgeoisie, and on the other by a traditional food-producing sector made up of semi-proletarians who cultivate basic grains but also depend on seasonal wage labour in the agro-export sector. According to this view, before 1979 the large agro-export bourgeoisie had used their influence on the state to displace the peasants from the potential cotton and livestock land and subsequently to prevent their access to the land on the agricultural frontier (Kaimowitz, 1986:104). The emerging dualism was considered to have been functional in creating a semi-proletarian labour force which could provide cheap seasonal labour and cheap food.

From this perception stemmed the emphasis on state farms and the attention to those sectors of production where the large agrarian bourgeoisie was dominant (ibid, 1986:107). The land confiscated from the Somozas was converted into state farms because this was seen as a continuation of large-scale, capital intensive farming brought about by the agrarian bourgeoisie. According to this interpretation, the bourgeoisie had achieved capital formation, modernisation and growth, and the state farms and the remaining agrarian bourgeoisie were expected to continue this role. Thus it was considered necessary to provide strong economic incentives to the agrarian bourgeoisie in order to stimulate them to continue production. On the other hand, this model required the continued existence of a semi-proletarian class to provide cheap seasonal labour to the agro-export sector and cheap food to urban areas. Thus redistributive land reform and real wage increases were perceived as inconsistent with this dualist model.

The opposing view argues that Nicaraguan agriculture cannot simply be defined as a two-sector, two-class model. Baumeister in particular states that the agrarian bourgeoisie is a less numerous class than is supposed in the dualist model. In his view there is a substantial middle class of medium-size producers. A class without much political influence and control of the state, but with a significant participation in export agriculture. As this class lacks the political power to create and reproduce a semi-proletariat, one can hypothesise that in his model this semi-proletarian class must be much smaller than in the dualist model. Baumeister and Vilas consequently interpret the trend in the development of the economically active population not only as one in which a substantial 'peasantry' has emerged, but also as one of increasing proletarisation. They call attention to the growing number of landless labourers who completely lost access to subsistence land. In their opinion the dualist model overestimated the role of the agrarian bourgeoisie and concomitantly of the semi-proletariat in agro-export activities.

The one-sided policy orientation towards the state farms and the large agrarian bourgeoisie has been detrimental for the recovery and the development of the agro-export sector. The state farms incurred substantial losses mainly because of the lack of experienced management. And the agrarian bourgeoisie, opposing the revolutionary process and its government, was not inclined to retake its role in capital accumulation. The foreign-exchange-intensive production methods of this class of producers and the over-generous credit provision it received from the government, made the incentive policies costly. At the same time the role of the medium-size farmers, of the family farms and of the rural proletariat has in their opinion been underestimated. Medium size producers and family farms require fewer incentives to produce and they have received less resources and government assistance than state farms and large capitalist estates.

Redistributive land reform that could have stimulated landless and land-poor small farmers was held up. And keeping down real wages contributed to labour scarcity, which became a serious problem in export agriculture. Kaimowitz (1986:113) argues that the 1985 switch in land reform policy, forced by the war situation, came late and does not represent a complete change in agrarian policies, as the government continues to invest substantial public resources in large scale projects.

As can be deduced from the presentation of the structure of the agro-export sector in Table 4.4, in this paper the simple two-sector, two-class model encompassed in the concept 'functional dualism' is not considered valid as a general characterisation of this sector. Small and medium-size producers participate substantially in export agriculture and this situation should have important implications for agrarian policies. The second model, which can be described as the 'farmer production model' better expresses this situation. It is evident that, at least up till 1985, the Sandinista policies have been one-sidedly inspired by the dualist perception. But that is not to say that the two models are mutually exclusive. In Section 4, for example, it will be argued with respect to coffee production that in Matagalpa/ Jinotega coffee is produced on large estates, still with a considerable participation of semi-proletarians, whereas in the Pacífico Central region, production is predominantly in the hands of medium-size and small farmers who hire a far more proletarianised labour force. Agrarian policies, in particular those related to labour availability for export crops, must take into consideration differences in structural characteristics and between crops.

In the following sections, labour problems in Nicaraguan export agriculture (Section 5) and in particular in the coffee sector (Section 6) are discussed. Fieldwork data are presented to place the labour process in the context of the regional production structure and to discern the different nature of the labour problem in various production zones.

4.   PRODUCTION SYSTEMS AND CLASS RELATIONS IN COFFEE-PRODUCING REGIONS

The two models which represent different perceptions of the Nicaraguan agrarian structure are useful to explain different tendencies in post-1979 agricultural policies. However, it seems that neither can fully describe Nicaraguan reality. For one thing, significant differences between crops and between regions can be observed.

In this chapter, regional differences in coffee production systems and its related class relations will be shown. One of the authors made a new elaboration of the coffee data of the 1980–1 LTC–CIERA survey which have formerly been elaborated on a national level by Havens and Baumeister (1983). He also participated in the ongoing research by the Department of Agricultural Economics of the UNAN on employment in the coffee sector in Nicaragua.[1] In this section production systems and class relations in the main coffee producing regions will be described. In the next section we shall elaborate on the consequences of regional differences in types of producer, as well as on the real possibilities of overcoming labour shortages by the various types of producer, which is currently a constraint on increasing coffee production.

In the Nicaraguan coffee sector there are three main producing regions. The departments of Matagalpa and Jinotega (Región VI) constitute the main region, with 52 per cent of national production in 1980–1 (UNAG–ATC–CIERA, 1982:23). The mountainous area of the Pacífico Central is the second area in importance. The departments in this area, Carazo, Masaya, Granada (part of Región IV) and Managua (Región III), account for 29 per cent of national production. The third area is the Interior Norte (Región I), consisting of Estelí, Nueva Segovia and Madriz, where 17 per cent of coffee was harvested in 1980–1. The agrarian structure and the man/land ratio are quite different in each region, which results in different labour relations.

Coffee production in the Pacífico Central takes place mainly on medium-size farms with a high degree of specialisation in coffee. On average 64 per cent of the land is under coffee; there are some other crops and a small area in pastures. Not much land is left unused at present, although the co-operatives have a high proportion of marginal land not yet incorporated into production (UNAN–DEA, 1987b:4). Over time the coffee farms have decreased in size. Production growth and capital accumulation are attained not by extension of the farm area, but by intensification of production, in particular by increasing yields of coffee cultivation. The 1986–7 survey data of coffee farms show a relatively high level of technology in this production region, which can be observed in Table 4.5.

Technical change in coffee production can imply different changes: renovation of the coffee shrubs, intensive pruning, use of fertilisers or

Table 4.5:   Technology level on coffee plantations by type of farm, Pacífico Central, 1986–7 (percentages)

Type of farm	Modern	Intermediate	Traditional	In development	Abandoned
Private farms	77	14	6	2	1
State farms	93	—	—	7	—
Co-operatives	76	2	19	3	—

SOURCE: UNAN–DEA (1987b:10).

Table 4.6:   Technology level on coffee plantations by type of farm, Matagalpa/Jinotega, 1986–7 (percentages)

Type of farm	Modern	Intermediate	Traditional	In development	Abandoned
Private farms	71	22	2	2	3
State farms	46	28	19	5	2
Co-operatives	12	37	—	6	44

SOURCE: See Table 4.5.

mechanisation of certain jobs such as irrigation, cultivation and spraying of chemicals. In this section attention will be concentrated on the level of technology, that is, on the use of certain varieties, pruning and biological–chemical inputs. The level of technology determines yields per unit of land. Coffee in the Matagalpa/Jinotega region is produced on large, traditional *haciendas* that combine coffee cultivation with livestock activities. There are some other crops and part of the land is unused.The degree of specialisation in coffee is low; on medium-sized and large farms the crop is cultivated on approximately one-quarter of the land. Expansion of the farm area is important for capital accumulation on most of these farms. As far as intensifying production is concerned this takes place by changing the product mix. First, unused land is transformed into pasture, and secondly, coffee trees are planted or other crops are grown on this land. As can be observed in Table 4.6, technology levels on coffee plantations are lower in this region than in the Pacífico Central. Labour shortages are a main obstacle for both maintaining technology levels and upgrading and renovation of coffee areas.

Table 4.7:   Social class characteristics of the labour force in coffee[a],
1980–1 (percentages)

Social classes	Pacífico Central	Matagalpa/ Jinotega	Interior Norte
Semi-proletarian	25	33	50
Agricultural proletariat	31	41	27
Non-agrarian labourers	44	26	23

SOURCE: Clemens (1987:21), based on 1980–1 survey among coffee pickers by LTC/CIERA.

NOTE: [a] Social classes are defined by allocation of family labour time. Semi-proletarians dedicated more than 10 per cent of family labour time to own cultivation and less than 50 per cent to wage work. Agricultural proletarians dedicated more than 50 per cent of family labour time to agricultural wage work. Non-agrarian labourers did the same with respect to non-agricultural work, either wage work or own account activities.

Therefore it is most important to analyse the labour situation in coffee production, taking into consideration the specific characteristics of the various production regions.

Table 4.7 indicates the class character of the coffee pickers by region. As can be observed in the Table, the 1980–1 survey found that semi-proletarian labour was less important in the Pacífico Central than in other coffee-producing regions. This is the most populated area of the country where agriculture is dominated by medium-size capitalist farms and in relative terms has been more modernised. Wage labour in coffee, according to the 1980–1 survey, was mainly supplied by proletarian labour, in particular by non-agricultural workers. The process of class differentiation in agriculture has advanced most in this region with, on the one hand, the formation of capitalist farms and, on the other hand, peasants losing access to land. As indicated above, coffee farms have decreased in size over time, but reached relatively high levels of specialisation and technology. The use of wage labour increased in this so-called farm production model. In this process of modernisation many peasants lost their land, or when they still had access to a subsistence plot they invested only a small part of family labour in it.

The 1980–1 survey shows that in the Matagalpa/Jinotega region semi-proletarian labour was more important than in the Pacífico Central. As indicated above, the large traditional livestock–coffee *haciendas* dominate agriculture in this region. Expansion of the farm area has been the characteristic way of accumulation of these *haciendas*. In that process peasants were reduced to a semi-proletarian status within the region itself or displaced to the frontier area of Zelaya, Boaco and Chontales from where they migrated to the coffee areas in the harvest season to earn a cash income. As Matagalpa/ Jinotega is the most important coffee region where half the crop is grown, labour demand in the peak season is substantial. The *hacendados* always had an interest in securing a labour supply for the coffee crop and they have been influential in the colonisation policy that contributed to the provision of semi-proletarian labour. In this sense the Matagalpa/Jinotega coffee region represents more the model of 'functional dualism', whereas the Pacífico Central can best be characterised as the 'farm production' model.

In the Interior Norte region half of the labour force in coffee production in the 1980–1 harvest consisted of semi-proletarian workers. In this area coffee is cultivated by small producers and semi-proletarian labour is provided by peasants from the same region who supplement their wage labour with growing basic grains. The Interior Norte contributes less to national coffee production than the other regions: only about one-sixth of the total. Coffee growers were less influential in pre-revolutionary government policy.

5. LABOUR PROBLEMS IN NICARAGUA'S AGRO-EXPORT SECTOR

With the low man–land ratio in Nicaragua, availability of labour power has been a long-standing problem in agriculture. However, through monopolisation of land by large landowners and the poor accessibility of a large part of the country, employers have succeeded in maintaining a sufficient supply of cheap labour-power. In addition, Salvadorean and Honduran migrant workers were contracted in times of peak demand, during cotton and coffee harvests. As a result, agro-export production could make use of cheap seasonal labour-power, furthering its expansion in the 1960s and 1970s.

After the triumph of the Sandinista revolution, policies towards the agro-export sector were directed at maintaining a high level of exports. But at the same time, measures were taken to improve the lot of the peasantry and to strengthen the position of the labour class by promoting their organisation. Growth of the agro-export sector could no longer be based on the existence of a labour reserve of peasants and landless workers with low incomes and lacking alternative employment opportunities, which forces them to offer their labour power on cheap terms. This contradiction is one of the central problems of Sandinista development policy.

As could be expected, and has happened in other revolutions, soon after 1979 labour shortages occurred in times of peak demand. Initially labour problems were most serious in cotton harvesting, but later the coffee sector met with even more problems. Several explanations for this situation have been put forward in the literature which are discussed by Weyland *et al.* (1988).

The explanations given by different authors depend on their perceptions of the rural labour market, which is reflected by the model of the Nicaraguan agrarian structure they follow. Initially, the Sandinista government, in accordance with the model of 'functional dualism', attributed labour scarcity to peasants who did not want to sell their labour-power, since the opportunities to employ this labour on their own plots had improved. Strengthening and reorganising the peasant sector by redistributive land reform and complementary policies would, it was believed, be detrimental to agro-export production.

The 'functional dualism' model stresses competition between wages in harvesting and peasant incomes on own plots. After an initial rise of wages in 1980, real wages in harvesting have fallen sharply compared to producer prices of peasant crops, as has been shown by Vilas (1984:401). The 'farmer production' model, in contrast, emphasises other factors to explain the labour shortage. Competition between wages in harvesting and non-agricultural incomes and other agricultural wage labour are stressed. Other factors are mentioned as well, such as labour productivity decline due to elimination of repression (Vilas, 1984:102, 348), and institutional factors like the loss of specific communication channels and intermediaries to recruit harvest workers (Colburn, 1983:15).

Irrespective of the two models, external factors have been important in the development of labour scarcity in the agro-export sector. Initially, labour supply decreased because international migration from Honduras and El Salvador ceased. Since 1983, the war has severely interrupted the functioning of the rural labour market.

When considering policies on wages and land reform, it can be concluded that cheap labour policies towards the agro-export sector have not disappeared since the revolution. However, because of falling labour productivity and rising opportunities for earnings in other activities, labour supply falls short of demand. Therefore cheap labour policies have in effect become an impediment to the growth, or even maintenance, of agricultural exports.

6.   LABOUR PROBLEMS IN COFFEE PRODUCTION

Comparison of survey results among coffee pickers in the Pacífico Central (1986–7) and the Matagalpa/Jinotega region (1985–6 and 1986–7) on large farms with 1980–1 data of pickers on large coffee farms, shows that in both regions participation of non-agricultural workers as well as of semi-proletarians has decreased (Aznar, 1986; Clemens, 1987; UNAN–DEA, 1987b; UNAN–DEA, 1987c). The agricultural proletariat is now the main source of labour for the coffee plantations, and to keep workers attached to the farm, producers are offering subsistence plots to permanent and even to seasonal labour.

In the Pacífico Central a slight reduction of semi-proletarian labour and a sharp decrease in the participation of non-agricultural workers can be noted. Real wages in coffee harvesting have not kept up with incomes from own-account activities of farmers and informal sector workers. Participation of informal sector workers, contributing 25 per cent of the total labour force, was quite important in this region during the 1980–1 harvest. It can be noted that most of them lived in rural areas or small towns and picked coffee in the municipality where they lived. It seems that, above all, rising profitability of trading and small industrial production, compared to wages in harvesting, have caused them to withdraw labour from coffee picking.

The 1985–(6) and 1986–7 survey in the Matagalpa/Jinotega region show a decrease in the participation of the semi-proletarian labour force, compared to the situation on similar sized farms in 1980–1. In that harvest season large private farms were still able to contract a relatively high number of migrant workers, most of them semi-proletarians, from agricultural frontier areas. On these farms 46 per cent of coffee pickers came from outside the department, compared to 28 per cent of coffee pickers on large state farms. Lower migration to state farms can be explained by the breakdown of traditional recruitment channels, in line with Colburn's argument (1983:15).

In the following years migration to large private farms decreased sharply as well, as a consequence of the reduced mobility of the frontier peasants. In the 1985–6 harvest, only 12 per cent of coffee pickers on large farms came from outside the department. The war situation makes seasonal migration to the coffee plantations more difficult. At the same time, competition between wages and food cultivation has turned against wages. Many peasants have also been evacuated from the war zones to the Matagalpa/Jinotega region and some have joined the agrarian proletariat, which now represents more than half of the labour force in coffee production. The participation of non-agricultural labour has decreased as was the case in the Pacífico Central. With respect to the Interior Norte region it should be mentioned that this region is most affected by the war. However, no recent survey data is available to document the changes in labour supply in this region.

The shortage of labour in coffee production, according to information provided by the producers, is more serious in the Matagalpa/ Jinotega area than in the Pacífico Central. The latter is more densely populated and less affected by the war. If a distinction is made according to type of farm, the survey data of 1985–6 and 1986–7 indicate that the large private farms are suffering most from the labour problem. State farms resolve their labour shortage in part by the employment of voluntary labour, the *brigadistas*. The co-operatives depend less on the hiring of wage labour because they make use of the employment of the membership and their families. In the Matagalpa/Jinotega region, however, the co-operatives have a high proportion of traditional coffee varieties with lower labour productivity, making it more difficult to hire labour when the same piece-rates are paid. Moreover, the co-operatives have received plantations with a high proportion of abandoned coffee land (see Table 4.6). To recover this area they actually need to invest more labour than under normal conditions, and therefore they have substantial labour problems too.

With respect to the traditional labour force in the coffee harvest there are some differences between the private farms and co-operatives on the one hand and the state farms on the other. The information in the 1985–6 survey indicates that private farms and co-operatives make use of personal relations to get in touch with outside labour. This results in the contracting of groups of workers, often formed by members of one family. The state farms have a more bureaucratic way of contracting labour; a larger proportion belongs to the agricultural proletariat, while more workers are hired individually instead of in groups. One of the characteristics of this agrarian proletariat, however, is that they spend more time on the coffee harvest than do non-agricultural or semi-proletarian workers. The state farms also contract more permanent labour which reduces their labour shortage in the harvest season.

The labour shortage is not only a problem in harvest time, but also in the slack season, when the coffee crop requires substantial care of a labour-intensive nature. The demand for labour in the slack season depends on the cultivation technology of the crop. Under modern conditions, three times more labour is needed than under traditional production methods, under intermediate conditions this factor is about two times. Labour input in the slack season is needed for pruning, irrigation and spraying of fertilisers and pesticides. On medium-sized plantations, wage labour must be hired for these tasks. In the present situation labour supply falls short of demand also in the slack season, which makes it difficult for producers to maintain the level of technology that has been reached. At the same time, investments in coffee renovation and in new plantations are low. As the lifetime of a modern plantation is about ten years, a substantial rate of substitution is required. The data in Tables 4.5 and 4.6 on the percentages of total area in development, indicate that investments are insufficient to replace older plantations, let alone to increase the acreage of coffee with modern cultivation technology. Large private producers retain investments because they lack confidence in the political and economic situation. But labour shortage in the slack season is an obstacle for investment for the state farms also.

As is the case with labour for harvesting the coffee, large private farms have most complaints about labour shortages in the slack season. That is, they have more difficulties in maintaining the level of technology and more obstacles for investment.

State farms have fewer problems in the picking season because they use voluntary labour, but although they employ proportionally more permanent labour than the other types of farms, they also suffer from labour scarcity in the slack season because the *brigadistas* are only available at harvest time. The co-operatives in Pacífico Central were the only ones reporting that they had no labour problem in the slack season. Yet the area they had in development at the time of the 1986–7 survey was small (see Table 4.5).

7. POLICY OPTIONS TO REDUCE LABOUR PROBLEMS ON COFFEE FARMS

The possibilities of overcoming labour problems and the prospects of adapting to the situation of labour scarcity differ by type of farm and by region. Large private farms have most difficulties in coping with labour shortages. They are less able to maintain their plantations and thus maintain productivity and are less willing to invest in renovation. Production will decrease gradually and so will labour demand. In the Matagalpa/Jinotega region where the degree of specialisation is low, producers are more inclined gradually to abandon coffee cultivation and to switch to other activities. In the meantime they make an effort to retain permanent and seasonal labour by providing them with a subsistence plot.

The state is counteracting the labour problems by the mobilisation of volunteers. Students and government workers are requested to pick coffee at some time, and since 1985–6 they are given material incentives. In the 1985–6 harvest nearly 20,000 *brigadistas* were mobilised compared to the employment of 41,400 traditional pickers; so they represented 32 per cent of coffee pickers. As their average productivity, however, is lower (3.1 tins per day, compared to 4.4 tins per day for traditional pickers), and the average picking period is shorter, their contribution to production was less, namely 12.4 per cent (UNAN–ULA, Gieskes and Valkenet, 1986:55). State farms get priority in their assignment, and for co-operatives and private farms relations with regional authorities are important for access to voluntary labour. In addition, state farms obtained more experienced volunteers, who picked for a longer period than those on co-operatives and private farms.

As stated before, the co-operatives, which have access to the labour of its members and their families, face fewer labour shortages. The co-operatives in the Matagalpa/Jinotega region in the process of land reform received marginal plantations with a high degree of traditional technology and a high proportion of abandoned coffee land. But the co-operatives in the Pacífico Central are in a somewhat better situation and they have no labour problem in the slack season. That makes it possible for them to invest in technological change and renovation of the coffee crop. For this to occur depends on the profitability of coffee cultivation compared with competing activities and on the pressure the members exercise to increase subsistence activities.

The situation on family farms has not so far been investigated sufficiently, but it is supposed that these can cope with labour problems in the same way as the co-operatives. Family labour can play an important role and personal relationships will be helpful in labour recruitment.

In the long run technological change is an important way to counteract labour problems. Higher labour productivity reduces the number of workers needed and provides the basis for higher wages. Labour productivity in the picking of modern varieties, if well pruned, is much higher than that of traditional varieties which predominate in Nicaragua. But as indicated, the present efforts in technological change and renovation are insufficient to produce such an increase in productivity. The state programme, CONARCA, has been criticised because of its large scale, low efficiency and the reduced participation of the farmers involved. It also employs a high proportion of the scarce technical personnel available in the country. It can be hypothesised that, because of their better access to the local labour market and to family labour, co-operatives and family farms would be better able to modernise coffee plantations and increase labour productivity than state farms and large private farms. These classes of producer would require sufficient support.

As has been stated, the role of semi-proletarian labour is already quite small in the Pacífico Central and is decreasing in the Matagalpa/Jinotega area. Land reform is not the cause of the relatively small contribution of semi-proletarians to labour supply on coffee farms. Upholding land reform, aimed at maintaining 'functional dualism', will contribute little to improving the labour shortages. On the contrary, in the short run, providing access to subsistence land seems to be a condition even for retaining the agricultural proletariat in the coffee sector. In the longer run, land reform which establishes co-operatives on coffee land may contribute favourably to resolving the labour problems.

8. CONCLUSIONS

After the Second World War Nicaragua experienced rapid economic growth led by the increase of agricultural exports. Expansion of export agriculture, in particular of cotton cultivation and ranching, displaced many peasants from their land, as had been the case in the past when coffee was established as an export crop. This process depressed the rural labour market, where cheap seasonal labour power became abundant and was hired in as cotton pickers and coffee harvesters.

After the revolution, the Sandinista regime aimed at maintaining a high level of agro-exports, but they were only partly successful.

Cotton production decreased to a lower level, as did coffee production from 1985 onwards. Minor export crops maintained their production levels, but beef exports fell sharply. Combined with falling export prices of agricultural products and rapidly decreasing industrial exports, this gave rise to a serious balance of trade deficit.

Even the lower production of cotton and coffee met with labour problems, especially in harvesting. Cheap labour policy continued, but among other factors, the increasing profitability of own-account activities, both in the informal sector and on own plots, led to a decreasing supply of seasonal labour power. Cotton picking was increasingly mechanised (reaching a level of 50 per cent of the total harvest in 1986–7), thereby further reducing its capacity to generate net foreign exchange. Coffee picking is dependent upon the mobilisation of voluntary labour that picked about 12 per cent of the relatively small harvest of 1985–6.

Labour availability has become a factor which impedes the expansion of agro-export production. This should be taken into account when policies are designed. Future prospects differ by product, by region and by type of producer. In this chapter, the case of coffee was examined. Although voluntary labour on this crop is useful in the short run to overcome the labour shortages in the harvest season, in the longer run the labour problem should be counteracted by productivity increases. In this respect labour shortages in the slack season are more serious because they make technological change and increases in labour productivity more difficult. Conditions for modernisation of technology and renovation of coffee plantations seem to be more favourable in the Pacífico Central than in Matagalpa/Jinotega due to the differences in the structure of the coffee sector in each region. In this respect, conditions seem more favourable for co-operatives and probably for family farms than for large private growers and state farms, especially because they have fewer labour problems in the slack season.

In the case of cotton the lower foreign-exchange margin which results from mechanisation is an important reason for the planned reorganisation of this sector. Cotton cultivation, which had expanded excessively, will be gradually restricted to areas with optimal conditions. World market prospects for sugar seem so gloomy that the intended expansion of sugar cane production may not take place. Beef production has not yet recovered and there is no information that large farmers are building up their herds. Internal consumption leaves a decreasing margin for export.

As most minor agricultural export crops seem to be largely produced by small farmers, it seems that expansion of these crops can be furthered by selective policies directed at small producers. Redistributive land reform can be compatible with policies to further agro-export production. First, allotment of plots to workers on large farms in the agro-export sector can help to retain labour on these farms, as was shown for the coffee sector. Secondly, land redistribution to small farmers individually or in co-operatives may well enhance their production of export crops, if additional policies are implemented. Credit policy, input provision, technical assistance and research for suitable innovations should be part of the package necessary to expand agro-export production in the stratum of small farmers.

Note

1. The Department of Agricultural Economics of the UNAN (UNAN–DEA) has conducted pilot studies in the coffee sector during the 1984–5 harvest. A large survey among coffee pickers and producers in the Matagalpa/Jinotega region was organised in the 1985–6 season. In 1986–7 surveys were held among producers and pickers of coffee in the Matagalpa/Jinotega region and in Carazo (Pacífico Central), as well as among cotton producers and pickers in León/Chinandega.

Bibliography

Aznar, P. (1986), *El Empleo en la Caficultura de la Sexta Región* (Managua: DEA).

Baumeister, Eduardo and Neira Cuadra, Oscar (1986), 'La Conformación de una Economía Mixta: Estructura de Clases y Política Estatal en la Transición Nicaraguense', in José Luis Corragio and Carmen Diana Deere (eds), *La Transición Difícil, La Autodeterminación de los Pequeños Países Periferícos* (Mexico: Siglo Veintiuno Editores).

Clemens, H. (1987), *Cortadores de Café en Tres Regiones Cafetaleras en Nicaragua (1980–81)* (Amsterdam: Vrije Universiteit).

Colburn, F. D. (1984), 'Rural Labour and the State in Post-Revolutionary Nicaragua', *Latin American Research Review*, XIX (3), pp. 103–17.

Colburn, F. D. (1986), *Post-Revolutionary Nicaragua: State, Class, and the Dilemmas of Agrarian Policy* (Berkeley, Cal.: University of California Press).

Havens, A. E. and Baumeister, E. (1983), *Recruitment and Retention of Occasional Workers in the Export Sector of Agriculture in Nicaragua*

(Wisconsin/Managua: Land Tenure Center, University of Wisconsin, and CIERA) (mimeo).

Kaimowitz, D. (1986), 'Nicaragua Debates on Agrarian Structure and their Implications for Agricultural Policy and the Rural Poor', *Journal of Peasant Studies*, 14(1), pp. 100–17.

Quirós, R. (1971), *Agricultural Development and Economic Integration in Central America* (Madison, Wis.: University of Wisconsin, Land Tenure Center).

SPP (1987), *Plan Económico 1987 – Colección Planes y Programas* (Managua: INIES/SPP).

Torres-Rivas, E. (1980), 'The Central American Model of Growth: Crisis for Whom?', *Latin American Perspectives*, 7(2), pp. 24–44.

UNAN, (1987a), *Datos Macro-Económicos de Nicaragua, 1960–1986* (Managua: Departamento Economía Agrícola).

—— (1987b), *Perfil de Productores de Café* (Managua: Departamento Economía Agrícola.

—— (1987c), *Encuesta de Cortadores IV Region, Dic./Enero 1986–87* (Managua: Departamento Economía Agrícola).

UNAG–ATC–CIERA (1982), *Producción y Organización en el Agro Nicaragüense* (Managua: CIERA).

UNAN–ULA, Serie Estudios (mimeograph).

Arts, D. and van der Schoot, T. (1985), *Aspectos Laborales de la Producción Cafetalera*, Serie Estudios no. 3.

Gieskes, Th. and Valkenet, P. (1986), *Los Brigadistas en el Corte de Café*, Serie Estudios no. 7.

Peschier, R. and van Ruyven, N. (1985), *La Oferta de Mano de Obra en el Tiempo de Silencio*, Serie Estudios no. 5.

Vilas, Carlos M. (1984), *Perfiles de la Revolución Sandinista* (La Habana: Ediciones Casa de las Américas).

Warnken, P. F. (1975), *The Agricultural Development of Nicaragua* (Columbia: University of Missouri Press).

Weyland, H. J. W., de Groot, J. and Buitelaar, R. (1988), 'Agrarian Transformation and the Rural Labour Market: the Case of Nicaragua', *Development and Change*, 19(1), pp. 115–37.

Williams, R. G. (1986), *Export Agriculture and the Crisis in Central America* (Chapel Hill N.C.: University of North Carolina Press).

5 A Comparative Study of the Salvadorean and Nicaraguan Cotton Sectors

Frans Thielen[1]

INTRODUCTION

Since the boom in cotton farming, this sector has played a vital role in the economies of Central America. Over the past decades, cotton-growing both in Nicaragua and El Salvador has brought economic development in terms of the generation of income, employment, economic infrastructure in the countryside, as well as the provision of foreign exchange. The effects of accelerating capitalist development in the countryside have been the expulsion of peasants from the cotton regions, their proletarianisation and marginalisation. In addition, the production of basic grains has diminished through the expansion of this agro-export sector, while cotton production has created less employment than it destroyed, and has been accompanied by bad working conditions and low wages.

On the other hand, cotton cultivation brought many benefits for a bourgeoisie who saw in its production and export new possibilities for the accumulation of capital. Both in Nicaragua and El Salvador the sector showed signs of economic concentration in the 1970s, although with different characteristics in each.

In the 1980s changes in the Nicaraguan and Salvadorean cotton sector were brought about by land reforms, the nationalisation of exports and the impact of civil wars. These have affected the possibilities for capital accumulation in both countries. In this chapter the structural changes of the cotton sector during the past two decades in the two countries will be compared, with emphasis on the development of the agrarian production structure and on the commercial systems. Conclusions will be drawn regarding the impact of these changes on the distribution of economic surplus within the cotton sector.

The first section reviews the background of cotton growing in both countries and its impact on socio-economic development. This is followed by an overview of the development of cotton production in the past. The following sections will compare recent changes in production and the commercial structure of this crop in Nicaragua and El Salvador, with special attention to the effects of the reforms implemented in the 1980s. The last section includes a résumé of the most important differences between both countries and some conclusions will be drawn regarding the way in which the reforms might have changed the distribution of economic surplus in each country.

1. COTTON BOOM AND CAPITALIST DEVELOPMENT

Cotton was one of the agro-export products which brought about a diversification of Central America's export agriculture during the 1950s. Before this, coffee and bananas were the major export commodities, coffee for more than a century, bananas for more than 50 years. Although cotton exports did not become important until the 1950s, cotton-growing had been going on for some time in Central America, mainly El Salvador, but almost exclusively for the local textile industry. When rising demand from foreign textile industries and the Korean War caused an increase in world market prices of cotton fibre, Central American cotton production was orientated to the world market.[2]

For Nicaragua the cotton boom was a turning-point in the development of the agricultural export sector. Before the 1950s, this country already had a diversified but backward economic development, which was reflected, for example, in the fact that less than a quarter of the potential agricultural land was used for production, and land yields and labour productivity were at a low level.[3] Compared with other Central American countries the incorporation of Nicaragua in the world market of primary goods took place rather late, as a result of the weakness of the local coffee bourgeoisie and the domination of the state by a traditional landed oligarchy. It was not until the decade of the 1890s that the coffee sector became important, whereas other Central American countries started in the 1870s. Coffee production rose significantly during the period 1920–40, but did not change the rural class structure, characterised by *latifundistas*, originally livestock farmers who later moved into coffee production.[4]

The introduction of cotton-growing broke with the historical pattern of development. It increasingly incorporated temporary labour, while eliminating subsistence farming which formerly had a complementary function for seasonal landworkers. Thus, cotton farming marks the full penetration of capitalism into the rural economy, specifically by the proletarianisation of the labour force.

The cotton sector began to develop in the 1930s and 1940s, when livestock farmers and merchants in the Pacific region became interested in alternatives for capital accumulation. They looked to sesame and cotton cultivation, rather than to other productive activities that arose during the Second World War, such as mining, lumbering and rubber cultivation which had an enclave character and were dominated by foreign investment.[5] In comparison with the Salvadorean case, which is dealt with later, the newly formed cotton bourgeoisie appeared to have weak interrelations with the dominant agro-export bourgeoisie at that time. Evidence of this can be found in Wheelock's historical work which analyses the formation of two economically powerful groups around the Bank of America (BANAMERICA) and the Bank of Nicaragua (BANIC). BANAMERICA emanated from the conservative oligarchy which originated in the eastern region, mainly Granada, and had economic activities in livestock, sugar cane and commerce. BANIC originally represented the interests of the rising cotton bourgeoisie and industrial sectors in the western region. On the other hand, the coffee bourgeoisie never formed a politically powerful group.[6] The economic group around BANIC developed interests in other economic sectors during the 1960s and 1970s.

The expansion of the cotton area was greatly stimulated by the active role of the Nicaraguan state in the process of capital accumulation. In a short period of time, the Pacific coastal plain was provided with an economic infrastructure by introducing electricity and building roads which facilitated access to land. A very crucial factor was the channelling of agricultural credits by the state banks.[7]

In a relatively short period the cotton area expanded from 23,000 manzanas of cotton (1 manzana = 0.7 ha.) in 1950 to a level of 123,000 in 1954 and reached a peak of 215,000 manzanas in 1965. In the same period, the participation of cotton fibre in the total value of exports rose from 5 to 45 per cent,[8] which made cotton exports more important for foreign exchange earnings than coffee over the next twenty years. In the 1980s cotton exports represented 20 to 34 per cent of total exports.

The cultivation of cotton also brought the modernisation of agriculture because of its intensive use of tractors, machinery, insecticides and pesticides. In the Pacific region, mainly the provinces of León, Chinandega and also, though less important, in Managua, Masaya and Granada, uncultivated land was brought into cotton production. A process of substitution of basic grains production took place. These were displaced to marginal land in backward regions with little economic infrastructure and less developed commerce, together with the migration of peasants to the lower Pacific regions.[9] In the peak years, 80 per cent of cultivated land of the Pacific coastal plain was dedicated to cotton production, resulting in a process of proletarianisation and concentration of land.

El Salvador had a different development before cotton fibre became a significant export product. Here an economically powerful agro-export bourgeoisie, based on coffee production, was formed in the second part of the nineteenth century. During the colonial period the Salvadorean agro-export sector was dominated for a very long time by indigo which was gradually displaced by coffee production in the past century. During this process, landlords and merchants had a great influence on state policy, which facilitated concentration and centralisation of land, brought about the elimination of the traditional peasant communities and made available the labour force necessary for the coffee sector. In the first part of the present century, the coffee sector was already highly concentrated. It was characterised by the presence of large coffee *haciendas* next to many small and medium-sized coffee producers, by a high level of concentration in the agro-industrial coffee mills, in coffee exports and the control of the banks by the coffee bourgeoisie. As a leading force of the dominant class in El Salvador, this coffee bourgeoisie had an oligarchic character.[10]

Before the fibre became a significant export commodity, cotton was cultivated on a small scale next to indigo during the colonial period. El Salvador possessed a local cotton craft industry composed of spinners and weavers who produced cloth for the domestic market. In the past century cotton was cultivated in the region around Olocuilta, Zacatecoluca and Usulután. But landowners and commercial farmers invested mainly in coffee, sugar and indigo plantations and not in cotton farms. This was due to the depopulation of the Pacific lowlands (a consequence of diseases in the colonial period which prevented human settlements there) and the competition of cheap cotton textiles from North America and Europe. In the first part of the twentieth century cotton was cultivated for the local market, encouraged by the establishment of a local, relatively modern textile industry in the 1930s, which by 1935 included four textile factories, increasing to 11 by 1950.[11]

The awareness of the potential importance of cotton as a raw material for local industries and as a valuable export commodity stimulated government attempts to encourage its production and organise its marketing through the establishment of the *Cooperativa Algodonera Salvadoreña* COPAL in 1940. The *Cooperativa* is a producer organisation to which, by law, all cotton growers must belong, and is the sole purchaser of cotton from the growers, owns the ginning industry and sells the crop both for domestic use and export. Compared with the Nicaraguan case, where cotton growers only had a regional organisation and poor relations with the already existing agro-export bourgeoisie, the cotton expansion in El Salvador was closely related with the coffee oligarchy. For this oligarchy, cotton was one of the new agricultural products appropriate for diversification of its economic activities.[12]

The Salvadorean cotton expansion took place more gradually than in Nicaragua. The cotton area increased from 27,000 manzanas in 1950 to 65,000 in 1955 and 162,000 by 1963, but it did have similar effects on the coastal plain, particularly in the provinces of La Paz and Usulután where most of the production was concentrated. Subsistence farming disappeared and the production of basic grains decreased sharply in the 1950s and 1960s. Browning[13] gives a detailed description of the process of displacement of the small peasants and large livestock *haciendas* by cotton cultivation and of its consequences for the Pacific region. It provoked the migration out of this region. The mechanisation of cotton production, except for harvest activities, meant that cotton growing did not offer sufficient opportunities for work and income to replace the decreasing possibilities for basic grain production. For El Salvador a very particular consequence of the expansion of cotton was the elimination of the last fertile land of the agricultural frontier. Unlike Nicaragua, cotton exports had less importance in the total exports of El Salvador. In the 1970s the share of cotton in total exports was nearly 15 per cent, in the 1980s less than 10 per cent.

2. THE DEVELOPMENT OF COTTON PRODUCTION IN NICARAGUA AND EL SALVADOR

The development of cotton production as an export commodity followed a similar pattern in Nicaragua and El Salvador. Figures 5.1,

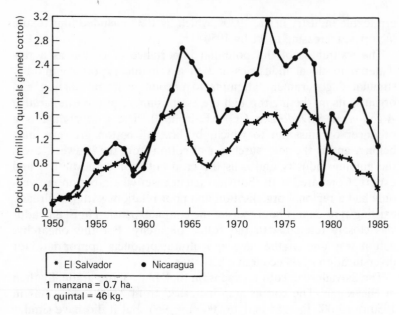

Figure 5.1   *Nicaragua and El Salvador: cotton production, 1950–85*

5.2 and 5.3 provide an overview of the development of production, area and yield in both countries.[14] In the past 35 years different time periods or phases of development can be distinguished, each having its own characteristics.[15]

The first period, from the beginning until the end of the 1950s, can be characterised as a *period of learning*. In that period, in both countries, several stimulating measures were undertaken, such as the creation of an adequate infrastructure in the Pacific regions and the granting of almost unlimited credit facilities for the sector. In Nicaragua the acreage of cotton increased rapidly from 23,000 manzanas in 1950 to 123,000 in 1954. In El Salvador the area expanded less, from 24,500 manzanas in 1950 to 76,000 in 1958 (see Figure 5.2). This difference in growth can be explained, among other reasons, by the fact that in El Salvador the construction of roads on the coastal plain of the Pacific proceeded more slowly than in Nicaragua.

Growth in the first part of the 1950s was stimulated by the high world market prices at the time, which decreased in the second half of the decade. The difference in yield of both countries in that period is striking (see Figure 5.3). Nicaragua obtained a yield of 7.6 quintals of ginned cotton per manzana (annual average, 1950–9), El Salvador

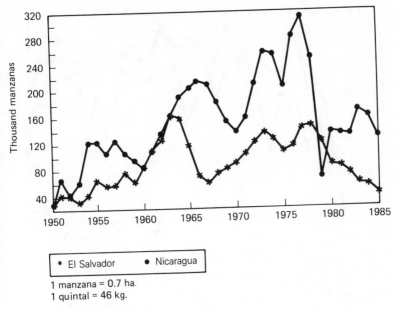

Figure 5.2   *Nicaragua and El Salvador: cotton area, 1950–85*

10.1 quintals, reflecting the positive effects of COPAL in stimulating improvements in cultivation techniques. In Nicaragua the low yield, together with the decreasing world market price in the second part of the 1950s, caused the first crisis in the cotton sector. It led to government intervention in the banks' credit facilities for cotton-growing. In the first years of the 1960s credit facilities were made conditional in order to stimulate modernisation of cotton-growing through the intensive use of insecticides and pesticides, and the mechanisation of land preparation and of the harvest.[16]

A second period was characterised by the *modernisation* of the sector in both countries, which was mainly carried out in the first half of the 1960s. The massive use of pesticides was introduced and mechanisation took place. An industry for the processing of cotton and sub-products and for the production of pesticides was created too. In this period the cotton acreage expanded rapidly, stimulated by increasing world market prices. In El Salvador the area more than doubled from 60,000 manzanas (in 1959) to 162,000 in 1963, in Nicaragua from 81,000 manzanas (1960) to 215,000 in 1966. In both countries the expansion took place mainly on land less appropriate

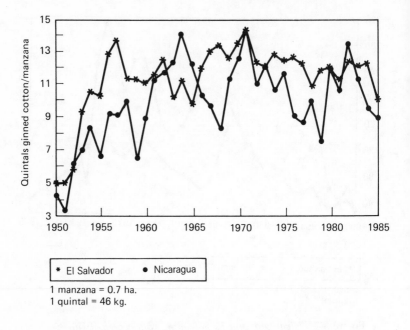

1 manzana = 0.7 ha.
1 quintal = 46 kg.

Figure 5.3   *Nicaragua and El Salvador: cotton yield, 1950–85*

for cotton-growing, and the period saw many small farmers begin to grow cotton.

A third period, from the mid-1960s until the end of the 1970s, shows a *consolidation* of the cotton sector. Although in El Salvador *concentration* already existed from the early period of cotton production, in Nicaragua it was mainly in this third period that concentration took place in production, in agro-industrial activities and cotton commerce. This will be demonstrated in the following sections.

In the second half of the 1960s, decreasing world market prices and productivity problems affected the development of the cotton sector. In El Salvador the cotton area was reduced to approximately 80,000 manzanas in 1969, in Nicaragua to 136,000 in the same year.

But at the beginning of the 1970s, as a result of rising international prices, a new period of euphoria in cotton growing began, mainly in Nicaragua where production doubled from 1.5 million quintals of ginned cotton (in 1968) to 3.2 million quintals (1973). Here the cotton acreage reached a new peak level of 259,000 manzanas in 1973 and 310,000 manzanas in 1977. As in the 1960s the expansion took place on inferior land and consequently had a low yield of 9 quintals of ginned cotton as an annual average in the second half of the 1970s. In El Salvador the cotton area increased to 146,000 manzanas in 1978, but maintained a higher level of average yields in comparison to Nicaragua.

In the next period, the 1980s, cotton growing was characterised by *restructuring* in both countries. Land reform programmes changed the production structure by creating state farms and a co-operative sub-sector in Nicaragua, and a co-operative sector in El Salvador. Nevertheless, during these years the development of production differed markedly in each country. After the sharp setback in 1979, caused by the war activities, cotton cultivation in Nicaragua continued at a level between 125,000 and 167,000 manzanas. The government made considerable efforts to stimulate cotton production notwithstanding low world market prices, increasing production costs and unfavourable conditions for cotton-growing resulting in sharply declining yields after 1982.

In El Salvador cotton production decreased continuously after 1978. In 1986 the cotton area was 23,000 manzanas; in other words, production had fallen to the level of the 1940s. The civil war in the countryside and the land reform programme were responsable for this to a greater extent than the unfavourable world market.

3. THE DEVELOPMENT OF THE PRODUCTION STRUCTURE IN NICARAGUA

In the 1950s and 1960s the development of very large cotton plantations like those in El Salvador and Guatemala did not take place in Nicaragua. This can be explained by the influence of the clan around Somoza, who did not permit a strong economic concentration of large *algodoneros* outside its control. Investments in cotton production were carried out by a bourgeoisie who did not have much presence in the agro-industrial phase of the cotton sector, nor in the domestic marketing, export and the financial activities of the sector. The most important bank for the sector after the first crisis, the Banco Nacional de Nicaragua, was controlled by the state. In fact, the sector was dominated by capital which did not have much presence in the sphere of direct agricultural production itself. Although cotton producers existed with a strong vertical integration, these were more the exception than the rule.[17]

Table 5.1:   Nicaragua: the distribution of cotton producers by size,
1963–71 (%)

Size of producer (manzanas)	1962–3			1971			
	Area	Production	Yield[a]	Number	Area	Production	Yield[a]
<10	2.2	1.6	76	27.4	1.6	0.9	57
10–50	8.9	7.4	83	35.8	7.2	4.4	62
50–500	59.8	60.2	102	31.7	54.7	52.3	96
>500	29.7	30.7	103	5.1	36.5	42.4	116
national[b]	137.4	100.0	32.7	2888	136.3	100.0	12.7

SOURCE: CEPAL/FAO/OIT (1980) pp. 61, 163; Warnken (1975) pp. 31, 33.

NOTES: [a] Index (national = 100); [b] Area in manzanas, yield in quintals per manzana unginned (1963) and ginned (1971).

Concentration in production mainly took place in the second part of the 1960s. In 1963 the sector included 3,676 cotton growers with an average size of 26 manzanas. In 1971 this number was reduced to 2,888 producers with an average size of 47 manzanas per producer, while the total cotton area had a similar dimension of 136,300 thousand manzanas[18] (see Table 5.1).

In this period many small producers disappeared because of their vulnerable position, reflected in low yields, due to their low use of new technology such as pesticides and insecticides, and lesser mechanisation of agricultural activities. Medium-sized and large producers, however, show a high degree of mechanisation and a homogeneity in the degree of use of technology. In 1963 the medium-sized and large cotton-growers, with more than 50 manzanas, obtained an estimated 25 per cent higher yield than the producers smaller than 50 manzanas (see Table 5.1). In 1971 these differences had increased, with relatively lower levels for small growers and higher yields (16 per cent above the national average) for the large ones (>500 mzs.). This is also explained by the small producers' limited access to bank credit, which made them more dependent on individual private financiers, and their use of predominantly rented land, much of it less appropriate for cotton cultivation.[19]

In this period the sector was dominated by medium-sized and large producers, who had a share of more than 90 per cent in total production, and concentration of production increased notably. During the period from 1963 to 1971 the share of very large pro-

Table 5.2: Nicaragua: the distribution of cotton producers by size,
1970–85 (%)

Size of producers (manzanas)	1970–1	1977–8	1978–9	1980–1	1983–4	1984–5
	Cotton area					
1–30	11.5	12.7	11.1	10.5	15.5	17.9
30–100	15.1	17.3	16.0	13.4	11.4	11.4
100–300	27.1	31.7	31.3	28.6	15.6	15.1
>300	46.2	38.3	41.6	47.5	48.2	44.9
Not classified[a]					9.2	10.8
Total ('000 mz.)	136.3	303.4	248.2	134.7	163.6	159.0
	Number of producers					
1–30	70.0	69.4	68.1	71.1		
30–100	16.2	16.7	16.8	14.2		
100–300	9.0	10.2	10.8	10.6		
>300	4.8	3.6	4.3	4.1		
Total (abs.)	2456	6442	4471	2172		

SOURCE: CONAL (1973); Banco Central de Nicaragua (1977) p. 20; Banco Central de Nicaragua (1978b) p. 91; Baumeister *et al.* (1983) p. 78; Evans (1987) appendixes 5 and 6.

NOTE: [a] The production co-operatives which in the statistics of MIDINRA normally are classified as small producers.

ducers in production increased from 30.7 per cent to 42.4 per cent. In 1971 there were nine cotton-growers with an average size of 1,510 manzanas and 31 with an average size of 691 manzanas. Yet medium and large producers (from 50 to 500 manzanas) together held the largest share in the cultivated area, which declined slightly from 59.8 per cent in 1963 to 54.7 per cent in 1971.

Analysing the development in the 1970s, when the acreage of cotton more than doubled within seven years, one finds that the relative shares of the different classes of producer remained fairly similar (see Table 5.2). Nevertheless, the total amount of cultivated land in cotton under the control of very large producers increased by 36,000 manzanas between 1970 and 1977 and by 1977 their number was 97. This class of producers with at least 1,000 manzanas cotton-land carried out their expansion mainly on leasehold properties.[20]

During this period the medium-sized producers (between 30 and 300 manzanas) appeared to be the most dynamic class, with their share in the total cotton area increasing from 42.2 to 49.0 per cent, from 57,000 (1970) to 148,000 manzanas (1977). This development in the 1970s represented not only a large concentration of land in the Pacific region, but also reflected the capacity of the medium and large producers to attract credit facilities from the banks, as well as inputs and technical services.[21]

After the victory of the Sandinistas in 1979 the policy of transformation in the cotton sector was characterised first, by an attempt to reactivate the sector following a setback in 1979–80, and secondly, by a restructuring in order to redistribute the economic surplus. The reforms which affected the cotton sector were mainly the nationalisation of the banks, exports and the land reform.

One of the first measures of the land reform was the expropriation of cotton land in the possession of large landowners who were closely associated with the Somoza family, and cotton land in the hands of large landowners which had to be expropriated due to political pressure at the time.[22] The magnitude of these expropriations is estimated at 17 per cent[23] of the cotton acreage (or 22,800 manzanas), and affected approximately half of the large cotton producers (over 500 manzanas). These large farms were thought to be of crucial importance for their share in total cotton production and export. Because of lack of confidence in the system of production co-operatives for this kind of property, they were brought under state control as *Unidades de Produccion Estatal* belonging to the *Area de Propiedad del Pueblo*. A further step in the land reform was the promotion of co-operatives among the small producers. Several measures were taken for stimulating the formation of co-operatives, such as the provision of agricultural credits on favourable terms.[24]

In the so-called second phase of the land reform which started in August 1981 (Decree 782), land property of any size efficiently cultivated by the owner was guaranteed, while land on holdings of over 500 manzanas which was not efficiently farmed, left idle or under-utilised could be expropriated, as well as properties of more than 50 manzanas in sharecropping and labour service arrangements.[25]

Besides the land reform, many other measures affected the development of the cotton sector. For example, the practice of land rental was important. Landlords who were not expropriated were forced to renew their rent contracts yearly and bound to a fixed maximum rent per manzana. This measure eliminated the existing usurious rents and gradually reduced the proportion of rental land in the cotton sector.[26] Several state enterprises were formed in the field of inputs

Table 5.3:   Nicaragua: the development of the cotton area and yield
according to the class of producer, 1980–5

	1980–1	*1981–2*	*1983–4*	*1984–5*
Area ('000 manzanas)				
Co-operative and small producers[a]	12.5	15.2	40.4	45.5
Private producers[b]	99.4	92.1	77.0	69.3
State producers[c]	22.8	25.4	46.2	44.2
Total	134.7	132.7	163.6	159.0
Yield (quintals unginned/manzana)				
Co-operative and small producers[a]			33.0	28.6
Private producers[b]			38.3	30.5
State producers[c]	38.4	34.9	28.6	27.3
Total	36.2	30.7	34.2	28.1

SOURCE: Baumeister *et al.* (1983) p. 78; Evans (1987) p. 10 and appendixes 5
and 6.

NOTES: [a] Includes peasant production (smaller than 30 manzanas), the
Sandinista Agricultural Co-operatives (CAS) and the Credit and Services
Co-operatives (CCS);
[b] Private production (larger than 30 manzanas),
[c] Also called Area de Propiedad del Pueblo (APP).

and technical services. Two examples are ENIA, which imports
agricultural inputs and is the sole importer of the base materials
needed for the production of pesticides and insecticides, and PRO-
AGRO, which distributes agricultural inputs to the state estates and
the co-operative sector. The state handles roughly 60 per cent of the
imports and approximately 40 per cent of the domestic trade in
agricultural inputs for the cotton sector.[27] It regulates the prices of
these inputs and also salaries, so that production costs in a great part
of the sector can be controlled by the state.

Table 5.3 gives an overview of the development of the sector in the
1980s. Here a distinction has been made between the class of small
producers (less than 30 manzanas) and co-operatives, the private
sector (with an area larger than 30 manzanas cultivated with cotton)
and the state enterprises. The cotton area of the co-operatives and
small producers increased from 12,500 manzanas in 1980 to 45,500
manzanas in 1984–5 or from 9 per cent to 28.6 per cent of the total
cotton area in four years. In 1984–5 the Sandinista Agricultural
Co-operatives (CAS) had a 38 per cent share in this area, the Credit
and Services Co-operatives (CCS) 49 per cent, and individual

peasants 14 per cent. The increasing share of small producers (at 17.9 per cent, mainly in the CCS) is remarkable, compared with their role in the 1970s, when the share of the small cotton growers in the total area amounted to just over 10 per cent (see also Table 5.2). This is one of the results of the government's policy of stimulating cotton-growing by small producers and their participation in co-operative production.

The area under the control of the state enterprises nearly doubled from 22,800 manzanas in 1980 to 44,200 manzanas in 1984–5 and their share increased from 16.9 per cent to 27.8 per cent. The private cotton producers, mainly the medium-sized and large growers, show a declining share, from 73.8 per cent to 43.5 per cent.

This data, together with that of Table 5.2, indicates a sharp reduction in the number of cotton growers between 100 and 300 manzanas. In the second half of the 1970s these medium-sized and large growers held almost one-third of the total cotton area in production; after harvest year 1982–3 their share declined to approximately 15 per cent in 1984–5. In other words, within two years some 13,000 manzanas cultivated by this class of producers had disappeared. Possibly many of them stopped growing cotton after the heavy losses in harvest year 1982–3.[28] Their properties may have been confiscated under the second phase of the agrarian reform, which would explain the huge growth of the state (APP) and co-operative sectors (principally the CAS).

The explanation for the continuing role of the private sector in cotton production, with control of nearly half of production, can be found in the dual policy of the Sandinista government towards private cotton-growers. The state sector does not have the capacity to assume total cotton production for reasons such as the lack of experience in cotton-growing and capable personnel, the relative inefficiency of state farms because of bureaucracy, and so on. Therefore the government first stimulated private farming in this sector by keeping it profitable (the introduction of guaranteed prices, extra incentives through the provision of foreign exchange for the cotton-growers, total finance for cotton production, and so on). Secondly, several measures have been taken to prevent private cotton-growers from decapitalising their farms and to prevent private growers from obtaining extraordinary profits from cotton-growing, trading or leasehold properties.[29]

Available figures from the cotton sector show that general tendencies in yields do not differ very much from those in the past. In the

1970s, the medium-sized and large cotton growers obtained higher yields than the small producers, explained by their unfavourable position in the cotton sector. In recent years too, the private sector, which mainly consists of medium-sized and large producers, obtained higher yields, 38 quintals in 1983–4 and 30 quintals in 1984–5 of unginned cotton per manzana (see Table 5.3). The co-operatives obtained 33 and 28 respectively, and the state sector 28 and 27 quintals per manzana in the same years.[30]

Observed differences in yield of the different types of producer cannot be explained unambiguously. Production conditions for cotton-growing have been somewhat deficient in recent years. The infrastructure for cotton-growing functions poorly, there is an in-adequate supply of crucial insecticides and pesticides, and a bureau-cratic tendency within the state institutions which work closely with the cotton sector, like AGROMEC (the supply and loan of machin-ery), ETSA (applications with aeroplanes), and others. These factors appear to have affected state farms and the co-operative sector particularly badly. In the case of the state enterprises, additional factors are the organisational problems, a lack of know-how com-pared to the private sector which has been cultivating cotton for years, and decreasing labour productivity caused by diminishing labour pressure and by an absence of repression.[31] The co-operative sector also has little experience of cotton-growing, which has not been compensated for by adequate support from MIDINRA and her institutions. Nor does the credit policy of the banks encourage a maximum harvest.[32]

This analysis makes it clear that since 1979 the Nicaraguan cotton bourgeoisie has not been able to continue its highly profitable activi-ties in the cotton sector. The gains from rented land have been limited. The provision of private credits have been practically elimin-ated because of the 100 per cent financing of cotton production by the state banks. In addition, the organisation of land workers, reduction of labour time, higher salaries and frequent labour unrest for better working conditions have influenced profitability rates. The policy of stimulating cotton growing also brought net losses of foreign currency for the state after 1984–5, caused by the subsidised low prices for cotton inputs and by the decreasing world market prices for the fibre.[33] This raises questions about the policy of stimulating cotton-growing at any cost. Meanwhile the private sector will prob-ably continue to produce cotton because of the absence of serious alternative production possibilities.

4. THE STRUCTURE OF PRODUCTION IN EL SALVADOR

By 1950, when the sector still had a modest size of 24,500 manzanas, large cotton-growers already dominated the cotton sector, a situation which developed in Nicaragua in the 1960s. Of the total area planted with cotton in El Salvador, 63.7 per cent was controlled by large producers, whose share increased by 1961 to 74.1 per cent of a total of 62,700 manzanas. On the other hand, many small producers were also cultivating cotton, but their participation was small: 9.6 per cent in 1950. This decreased to 4.9 per cent by 1961.[34]

This early concentration of production can be explained by the fact that these producers originated from a fraction of the large landowning bourgeoisie that looked upon the cotton sector as a possible alternative to diversify investments. Cotton production had more risks than coffee production, but capital had a higher velocity of circulation because of the short lapse of time between the seeding and harvest time. For the large landowners the cotton sector also extended the possibilities for land rental.[35]

A characteristic feature of cotton production during the 1960s was the frequent use of leasehold properties, particularly among small producers rather than medium-sized and large producers. Historically, the land of better quality was owned by the large landholders. So cotton expansion in the first part of the 1960s took place on marginal land,[36] mostly leasehold properties, by small farmers and even by *minifundistas*. For example, in the peak year 1964 the sector numbered 2,873 small producers with a share of 15.9 per cent of the total area, of whom 79.3 per cent cultivated cotton on leasehold properties.[37]

Table 5.4 summarises the development of producers by size in the period from 1964 to 1978. The data for harvest year 1969–70, when the total cotton acreage (79,800 manzanas) was comparable to that of 1961, show few shifts in the share of different classes of grower. In 1961 the share of large producers (larger than 100 manzanas) amounted to 74.1 per cent, by 1969–70 it decreased to 68.5 per cent and in 1978–79, when the total cotton area was doubled to 150,000 manzanas, it was 66.5 per cent.

A comparison with Nicaragua leads to the conclusion that in this period the structure of production, measured by the share of the different classes of producer, is comparable. For example, in El Salvador 17.8 per cent of the total number of producers controlled

Table 5.4: El Salvador: the development of the cotton sector by size of producers, 1964–78

Size of producer (manzanas)	1964–5		1969–70		1978–9	
	Number (%)	Area (%)	Number (%)	Area (%)	Number (%)	Area (%)
<20	62.9	15.9	65.9	10.3	62.3	10.6
20–50	20.5	15.8	16.4	9.3	21.4	11.7
50–100	7.9	13.1	7.3	11.9	8.2	11.1
100–300			7.2	26.1	7.2	21.7
300–500	7.6[a]	35.0[a]	1.5	11.8	1.5	18.1
>500	1.0	20.2	1.7	30.6	1.1	26.7
Total (abs.)	4564	158.5	1883	79.8	2764	150.6

SOURCE: Browning (1975) p. 371; Arias (1984) p. 29; Hernández (1980) p. 12.

NOTE: [a] Includes data from producers with a size of 100 to 300 manzanas.

68.5 per cent of the area (in 1969); in Nicaragua 13.8 per cent of the total number of producers controlled 73.3 per cent of the area (1970). In El Salvador at the end of the 1970s, 10.9 per cent controlled 66.5 per cent of the area, and in Nicaragua 15.1 per cent of the producers controlled 72.9 per cent of the area.

The data from the 1970s also shows the small and medium-size producers in the same role as in the 1960s. In times of conjunctural growth in the cotton sector, their numbers increase rapidly, and in periods of temporary crisis the contrary will happen. In 1969 the sector in El Salvador numbered 1,240 small producers, a number that increased to 1,723 in 1978 when the cotton area had doubled and the peak level of production of the middle of the 1960s had nearly been reached. However, their share in the total acreage remained almost the same: about 10 per cent. A comparable increase in the number of medium-sized producers, from 446 to 739, could be observed.[38] In comparison with the Nicaraguan case, few small and medium-size producers in El Salvador had been brought into production in the period of growth during the 1970s.

Geographically speaking, the cotton sector is principally located in three coastal provinces, in order of importance, Usulután, La Paz and San Miguel, where 79.1 per cent of the production is concentrated. The character of the production structure is different in each province. In Usulután and San Miguel there are many small

Table 5.5: El Salvador: the most important families operating in the cotton sector and their other economic activities, 1972–3

Family	Cotton[a] Production 1972–3	Coffee[b] Production 1970–1	Coffee Export 1973–4	Sugar[c] Production 1973–4	Sugar Export 1973–4	Land property (ha.)	Economic activities related to the cotton sector
Wright	226.0				250.0		Insecticidas de El Salvador; Textilera del Pacífico; Productos Agroquímicos de C.A.; RAIT, S.A.
Dueñas	124.0	45.5	76.0	44.0	52.0	6424	
Kriete	100.0	13.0	13.0			810	
García Prieto (Salaverría)	92.0	20.0	168.5				Textiles Tazumal; Textiles del Pacífico
Cristiani	79.0	12.5	57.5				Industrias Químicas; Semillas, S.A.
Hill	77.0	49.5	37.5			102	Textiles Tazumal; Textiles del Pacífico
Guirola	67.0	72.1		9.0		13682	Chemical Industries
Dalton	35.0	21.5	11.0			1480	
Duke	34.0	5.5	7.0			535	

Salvaverria	31.0	31.5	152.5	10.0		7808	Importation of Fertilizers
Homberger	29.0	6.0	48.0			1018	Industrias Agrícolas Ideal; IAISA; Semillas, S.A.
Llach-Schonenberg	27.0	50.0	93.0			117	
Borgonovo	22.0		119.0				
Nottebhon	18.0				60.0		Textiles Tazumal; Textile Industry
Avila Meardi Palomo	18.0	19.0	23.5	25.0			
Daglio	18.0	35.5	231.0			1869	Chemical Industry
López-Harrison	14.0		7.0	250.0			Insecticidas de El Salvador
Eduardo Salaverria	10.0	12.0	41.5	10.0			
Papini	8.0						Chemical Industries

SOURCE: Colindres (1977) Table 67 (appendix).

NOTES: [a] Production in '000 quintals unginned cotton.
[b] In '000 quintals processed coffee.
[c] In metric tonnes.

producers as well as a great number of very large producers, while in La Paz there are relatively few small ones but many large producers.

The preceding analysis of the distribution of areas and production does not demonstrate sufficiently the highly concentrated character of this Salvadorean agro-export sector. This concentration can also be observed outside the agricultural phase of the cotton sector, namely, in the supply of inputs, the private credit facilities, the industry associated with the cotton sector, the intermediary trade of cotton, and in the other economic activities undertaken by the agro-export bourgeoisie outside the cotton sector. Table 5.5, composed from a study by Colindres, provides a detailed picture of 19 important Salvadorean families who controlled a quarter of cotton production in 1972–3 and have other enterprises both related to the cotton sector and outside it.[39] They are mostly large landowners who are also active within the production and export of coffee and sugar. This bourgeoisie has a presence in each phase of the cotton sector, from the supply of inputs and cultivation to the cotton-related industry. Table 5.5 could be extended to include other economic activities in which many have investments, such as banking, construction, transports, insurance, and so on.

The data on the cotton production of these families shows a higher degree of concentration than can be deduced from the data presented earlier. Many large landowners started to cultivate cotton on a family *hacienda*. When the first harvests appeared to be successful, they extended the cultivation of cotton to other farms, sometimes renting neighbouring *haciendas*, usually owned by related large landowners. For example, the three largest cotton families, the Wrights, the Dueñas and the Krietes all had *haciendas* in the centre of the cotton region in the coastal plain of the Pacific where the cultivation of cotton started.[40] Later, they expanded their activities as landlords, as granters of credit facilities, as suppliers of inputs, and especially as intermediary tradesmen of cotton.

The high amounts of cotton production of each family can only be explained through their purchase of great quantities of cotton. This was also illustrated by an investigation in 1978 which found that 310 producers who were authorised to cultivate 14,000 manzanas of cotton delivered 899,000 quintals of unginned cotton to COPAL. These producers obtained a technically impossible yield of more than 60 quintals of unginned cotton per manzana. This was partly obtained by the purchase of unginned cotton from others, often smaller growers.[41]

Leasehold properties in the cotton sector continued to be significant for the sector in the 1970s, especially for small and medium-sized cotton growers.[42] In 1969 56 per cent of cotton production was carried out on leasehold properties; in 1976 this had decreased to 39 per cent, while rents increased sharply, from 98 *colones* per manzana in 1969 to 200 in 1974 and 262 in 1981, a clear reflection of the concentration of land in the cotton areas.

Small and, to a lesser extent, medium-size producers, because of the smaller size of their properties and lesser financial capacity, have less access to bank credits.[43] The larger producers and landlords often use the bank credits for cotton production to finance the initial investments for other cotton growers, often accompanied by a leasing contract and a contract for the delivery of the cotton crop, which reflects the complex interrelationships that exist between small, medium-sized and large producers.[44]

The development of the cotton sector during the 1980s was greatly influenced by the crisis which began in 1979 and the reforms begun in 1980. These reforms were aimed at counteracting the effects of the exhaustion of the accumulation model of the 1970s. The main problems arose because of the inability of the labour force to reproduce itself and the increasing popular mobilisation against the repression of organisations and trade unions in the past.[45]

The land reform, and the nationalisation of the banks and exports, was the basis of the economic policy that was put into practice after 1980.[46] These policies had less direct effects on the cotton sector than on the other agro-export sectors. As distinct from coffee and sugar, the exports of the cotton sector were not nationalised because the producers' organisation, COPAL, already existed.

On the other hand, the land reform directly affected land distribution in the cotton sector. The basis is the Agrarian Reform Law (Decree 153, March 1980) that was to be executed in three phases. For the cotton sector phase I is of relevance, because it affects all holdings larger than 714 manzanas which are to be expropriated by the Salvadorean Institute for Land Transformation (ISTA). The expropriated landowners have the right to reserve between 142 and 214 manzanas of the expropriated property. Once the amount of compensation for the expropriated landowner is settled, ISTA transfers the *finca* to an agricultural co-operative that consists of the former rural workers and *colonos* of the holding.[47] The only land properties that are allowed to be larger are the agricultural co-operatives that were already established or were created after 1980.

Table 5.6:   El Salvador: the development of the cotton sector, 1980–5

	1980–1	*1981–2*	*1982–3*	*1983–4*	*1984–5*	*1985–6*
Area[a]						
Co-operatives	22.5	28.2	23.2	18.8	22.9	19.6
Private sector	60.6	54.6	48.1	35.6	30.6	19.8
Total	83.1	82.8	71.3	54.4	53.5	39.4
Yield[b]						
Co-operatives	34.5	31.8	33.7	34.7	30.9	23.7
Private sector	30.2	27.5	31.8	29.1	32.1	29.1
Total	31.3	29.0	32.4	31.1	31.6	26.4

SOURCE: COPAL (1985) p. 9; COPAL (1986) p. 6; ISTA (1985) p. 12.

NOTES: [a] '000 manzanas; [b] quintals unginned cotton/manzana.

As a result of the reform, a sub-sector of co-operatives was created on the basis of the expropriation of large land properties. In 1980 the total area of the co-operatives was 22,500 manzanas or 27 per cent of the total cotton area. Sixty-six co-operatives were established of which 60 are located in La Paz and Usulután, where the large land holdings in the sector are mainly found. Co-operative production has become more important; its share of the total area increased in 1985 to almost 50 per cent, principally as a result of the diminishing area of the private sector, from 60,000 manzanas (72.9 per cent) in 1980 to almost 20,000 manzanas in 1985 (50.4 per cent) (see Table 5.6).

The apparent retreat of the private sector from cotton production has several explanations. The civil war has affected the cotton harvest in the eastern coastal plain of El Salvador for more than nine years. Many private producers have accumulated debts with the banks, caused by the increasing prices of agricultural inputs and low prices for the cotton fibre, but also due to their capital exports in the first years of the 1980s. Before the nationalisation of the banks, the large producers had almost no financial problems because they had their own banks for credit facilities. Another explanation for the decrease of private production can be found in the threat of expropriation by the land reform programme, which led landowners to split large land properties into smaller ones with different owners, and which resulted in a decline in investment in cotton-growing by the agro-export bourgeoisie.[48]

The effect of splitting land properties within the cotton sector probably explains the shift that has occurred in the last ten years in

Table 5.7:   El Salvador: the distribution of the cotton area and
production according to the size of producers, 1969–82 (%)

Size of producers (in mzs)	1969–70			1982–3			
	Area	Pro-duction	Yield[a]	Area	Area of co-oper. sector[b]	Pro-duction	Yield[a]
<20	10.3	8.9	30.6	7.5	–	7.0	31.6
20–50	9.3	8.2	31.1	11.5	–	10.7	31.7
50–100	11.9	11.7	34.5	11.6	0.7	11.4	33.7
100–300	26.1	25.6	34.6	26.8	8.3	25.0	31.7
300–500	11.8	12.0	35.8	18.4	9.3	19.3	35.7
>500	30.6	33.6	38.7	24.2	16.2	26.5	37.3
Total[c]	79.8	2813	35.3	69.6	23.2	2366	34.0

SOURCE: Arias (1984) p. 29; MAG (1983) p. 36; ISTA (1985) pp. 15–19.

NOTES: [a] Quintals unginned cotton/manzana.
   [b] Share in the national cotton area, calculated from data of 1983–4.
   [c] Area in '000 manzanas, production in '000 quintals unginned
   cotton.

the distribution of land in the upper strata of the cotton growers. As
Table 5.7 shows, the share of the large producers with between 300
and 500 manzanas, increased from 11.8 per cent in 1969 to 18.4 per
cent of the total area in 1982, while the participation of the very large
producers (more than 500 manzanas) decreased from 33.6 per cent to
26.5 per cent. The major part of co-operative production can be
found in this class of producer, and the remaining large production
on leasehold properties.

As can be noted in Table 5.6, the co-operative sector obtained
higher yields in the first years of the 1980s. In 1980–1 these were 34.5
quintals of unginned cotton per manzana, compared with 30.2 quintals in the private sector. This tendency, maintained until 1983–4,
when the co-operative sector had a yield of 34.7 and the private
sector of 29.1 quintals, seemed to reflect the advantages of large-scale
production. The private sector, on the other hand, has many small
and medium-size producers which results in a lower average yield.
This can be seen in Table 5.7 where the distribution of area and
production according to the size of the producers is calculated and
compared with the distribution of the co-operative area according to
the size for 1982.

During the 1980s, the existence of leasehold properties remained characteristic for the sector; nearly 50 per cent of the cotton is still cultivated on leasehold properties.[49] A reason for the small tenant not claiming his right to land according to phase III of the land reform can be found in the fact that on many properties there are great debts, such as mortgages and so on, which the tenant has to take over when the property is transferred to him.

In recent years the small producers have tended to disappear. Their share in the total cotton area decreased from 10.3 per cent in 1969 to 7.5 per cent in 1982 (see Table 5.7). In 1969 their number was 1,240 with an average size of 6 manzanas, which increased to 1,723 in 1978 with an average size of 9 manzanas. However, data from 1985–6 suggest that the small producers with less than 20 manzanas have almost completely disappeared.[50] The crisis which the sector confronted during the 1980s and their unfavourable position compared with medium-sized and large production, have strongly affected the position of small producers.

This unfavourable position is reflected in the yields obtained. Producers with less than 50 manzanas obtained a lower yield in 1982–3 as well as in 1969 compared with the medium-sized and large producers with an area of more than 50 manzanas of cotton. The smaller producers obtained an average yield of 30.8 quintals of unginned cotton per manzana in 1969–70, unlike the average yield of 36.3 quintals for producers larger than 50 manzanas. In 1982–3 this difference continued, with a yield of 31.7 quintals for smaller producers and 34.6 quintals for producers larger than 50 manzanas (Table 5.7). This position of the smaller producers in the sector can be explained by the use of inferior land for cotton production, lesser access to banking loans, and the fact that they make less use of modern technology. The small producers have mechanised agricultural activities to a lesser extent than in the 1970s. For land preparation, 70 per cent use a tractor, but for the other agricultural activities they hardly use tractors at all (nearly 5 per cent of the cotton area). Producers with holdings larger than 50 manzanas make a lot more use of tractors: for land preparation 99 per cent, sowing 71 per cent and other agricultural activities 56 per cent of the cotton area.[51] These differences have continued during the 1980s.

5. THE COTTON TRADE IN NICARAGUA

Before the Sandinista revolution, trade structure provided both the local bourgeoisie and the foreign merchant houses many opportunities for appropriation of economic surplus in the cotton sector and for the realisation of extra profits obtained from offering credits, purchasing and selling cotton and from the trade in agricultural inputs.

Domestic trade and exports in Nicaragua had a more heterogeneous structure than in El Salvador. In the 1970s the ginning industry had 28 *desmotadoras* (cotton gins) and exports were in the hands of approximately sixteen trading companies.[52] Institutions with regulating functions in the marketing of cotton rarely existed. There was a *Comision Nacional de Algodon* (National Cotton Commission, CONAL) with a mainly advisory function to the government. It centralised information on the sector, carried out research on cultivation techniques, and was established in a period when many public institutions were set up to stimulate exports.[53] Within the cotton trade CONAL's function was to classify cotton, which often resulted in serious conflicts between producers and exporters.

The sales of cotton mainly took place through direct sales to (representatives of) international trading houses or to local intermediary merchants and had three forms: cotton-growers could sell their harvest to the processing industry which gins the raw cotton (the *desmotadoras*), to the middlemen or also to the two existing cotton co-operatives, Santa Ana and Esquipales.

Large cotton producers had more direct relations with export companies and middlemen to whom the cotton was sold mainly after it had been ginned by a *desmotadora*. Small and medium-sized producers did sell more of their crop in unginned form and mainly to the ginning industry and middlemen. Table 5.8 illustrates the heterogeneous character of cotton marketing and the different ways in which small, medium-sized and large producers sold their production in 1977–8. The middlemen had an important role in the cotton trade, because half of the ginned cotton (51 per cent) passed them first, mainly bought from large producers, before it was exported by a trading company. The ginning industry also had an important role, it bought 74 per cent of the sold unginned cotton production.

Contract selling was widespread among cotton-growers in the 1970s. Mainly small producers, but also some medium-sized and large producers, used the system of forward selling their crop, which

Table 5.8:   Nicaragua: destination of cotton sold by cotton-growers by size of producers, 1977–8 (%)

Size of producer (mzs)	Desmotadoras	Exporters	Merchants	Others	Total
	Unginned cotton				
0–25	3.5	1.0	4.6	2.9	12.0
26–100	11.8	2.3	7.7	2.1	23.9
101–200	10.5	–	0.7	4.4	15.6
>200	48.5	–	–	–	48.5
Total	**74.3**	**3.3**	**13.0**	**9.4**	**100.0**
	Ginned cotton				
0–25	0.1	0.1	0.7	0.1	1.0
26–100	0.7	1.1	1.7	0.6	4.1
101–200	–	1.7	1.6	0.6	3.9
>200	2.7	41.4	46.9	–	91.0
Total	**3.5**	**44.3**	**50.9**	**1.3**	**100.0**

SOURCE: Banco Central de Nicaragua (1977) appendix Table 33.

generally resulted in a lower cotton price in exchange for credit facilities. Middlemen operated not only as financiers of production but were at the same time suppliers of insecticides and pesticides.[54]

Although many merchants, export companies and the ginning industry were operating in the domestic intermediary trade, the export of cotton fibre had an oligopolistic character. As can be observed in Table 5.9, four export enterprises out of the sixteen cotton exporters controlled 54 to 76 per cent of the cotton exports in the 1970s. Núñez (1980) showed that the export companies were mainly controlled by foreign capital. From the total of sixteen trading companies, twelve were functioning as agents of international trading firms, of which eight had their headquarters in the United States.[55]

The oligopolistic character of the cotton export trade, the role of the middlemen, forward contracting combined with the credit facilities and with the supply of inputs for the sector, increased the contradictions between the cotton producers and the Somoza regime during the 1970s. The profitability of the small and middle-sized producers was affected by the low prices for cotton and increasing production costs (especially of inputs such as fertilisers and pesticides). The producers wanted the Somoza regime to introduce regulations for the domestic cotton market and stimulate cotton production. One of the severe problems was the instability of prices

Table 5.9:   Share of the four most important export companies in total cotton exports, 1975–9 (%)

Trading company	1975	1977	1978	1979
Comercial Azteca	21.9	27.2	30.5	43.6
Cottonimex	11.3	16.6	11.6	21.0
Uwe J. Lorenzen y Cía. Ltda.	12.0	9.6	3.9	3.5
Servicio Agrícola Gurdían S.A.	8.4	6.0	8.5	7.6
Total	53.6	59.4	54.5	75.7

SOURCE: Baumeister *et al.* (1983) p. 49.

and the great differences between the prices of cotton on the world market and local prices.[56] The producers wanted the creation of a kind of co-operative for the cotton trade, comparable with the Salvadorean COPAL. But the state preferred nationalised commerce.

However, the economic policy pursued during the 1970s increasingly affected the interests of the cotton producers because of the existing close relations between the Somoza regime and financiers, as well as trade and industry in the cotton sector and its entanglement with foreign capital which had little involvement in direct production. In harvest year 1973–4, for example, these contradictions resulted in the mobilisation of cotton producers in order to reopen negotiations on the low prices fixed by forward contracts. At that time the state intervened by decree, forcing the cotton producers to fulfill 70 per cent of their forward sales contracts.

After the Sandinista victory a state monopoly on the domestic trade and the export of cotton was established by the creation of the *Empresa Nicaraguense del Algodon* (ENAL). This eliminated the formerly flourishing intermediary trade in the sector and ensured that foreign exchange from cotton exports would go to the state. Today, the state controls prices at each stage of the sector, as well as exports and domestic sales of cotton and its sub-products.

In contrast with the Salvadorean situation, the domestic market for cotton in Nicaragua has little importance. The ginned cotton sold on this market is less than 10 per cent of the volume of total cotton production in the past (see Table 5.10). The textile industry has hardly been developed; in the 1980s this industry employed nearly 1,600 persons. Besides the textile industry, the oil industry plays an

Table 5.10:   Nicaragua: development of the domestic market and cotton
production, 1950–84

Period	Production[a]	Consumption[b] (%)
1950–9	664.3	2.9
1960–9	1814.6	3.3
1970–9	2265.7	4.3
1980	1645.8	5.1
1981	1387.4	4.0
1982	1753.2	4.3
1983	1884.5	6.9
1984	1505.6	8.5

SOURCE: Harness and Pugh (1970) p. 25; Banco Central de Nicaragua (1987a) p. 74; Comité Consultivo Internacional del Algodón (1986); and sources listed in Appendix 1.

NOTES: [a] '000 quintals ginned cotton.
[b] Consumption on local market as % of production.

important role. The cotton piths, one of the sub-products in the agro-industrial process of ginning cotton, is the main raw material. In the past ten years this industry processed about 90 per cent of the cotton piths and there are six enterprises which together employ more than 1,000 people.[57]

Since 1979, nine out of the 26 *desmotadoras* have become state property, while the rest of this industry is controlled by large producers or the oil industry. These *desmotadoras* function as storage centres and as the location where commercial operations take place (sales, deductions for quality, packing, and so on).[58]

Cotton sales for the most part take place in the form of ginned cotton. The cotton price is fixed at FOB prices at Corinto's export port, from which a fixed percentage is deducted for inferior cotton quality and for the cost of transport to the port. For several years a discussion has been going on about the fixed cotton price which represents a state subsidy for the cotton sector, while the official rate of exchange of the *cordoba* is used for the calculation of the cotton price in *cordobas*. This official rate does not reflect the rate of exchange on the parallel or black market that can be ten times above the official exchange rate.

During recent years prices have been adapted to make cotton production more lucrative for private cotton-growers,[59] a policy which reflects the importance placed by the Nicaraguan government on the stimulation of cotton production and on the resulting extra foreign currencies. Other measures taken are the introduction of a preferential rate of exchange of 15 *cordobas* per dollar (before this it was C$ 10) in 1982, the introduction of the right of cotton growers to purchase foreign currencies in 1983 and the partial payment of the harvest in dollars in 1985.

6. SALVADOREAN COTTON TRADE

From the time that cotton became important as an export product the co-operative COPAL played a central role in stimulating its cultivation. Originally the establishment of this organisation was meant to organise the smaller producers and to improve both cultivation methods and marketing possibilities of cotton, which was dominated from the beginning by a few industrialists. Because COPAL has always been controlled by larger cotton producers little remained of these original objectives and the co-operative became the principal means by which the Salvadorean agro-export bourgeoisie guaranteed their interests and profits in this sector.

COPAL has, by law, the monopoly of the local cotton trade, ginning and export. Also, it is the sole institution which can authorise the cultivation of cotton by individual producers and is the sole supplier of cotton seeds. It provides both technical assistance and inputs (such as fertilisers and pesticides) to the cotton growers. Farmers who desire to cultivate cotton have to join the co-operative.

A characteristic feature of COPAL is the almost complete domination of the board of directors by the large growers, who thus also strongly promote their interests in cotton production and trade. A detailed study shows the rotation of the membership of the board of directors during 1940–80 within a group of 122 persons, 33 of whom belonged to the category of medium-sized and large producers, and the remaining 89 persons can be considered members of the large producers category, coffee-farmers and industrialists.[60] An illustrative example is Juan Wright, a large landowner who possessed 5,900 manzanas of land during the 1970s, had a cotton production of 226 thousand quintals of unginned cotton (see also Table 5.5), had investments in trade companies, transport and banking, and was chairman of the co-operative for nine years.[61] According to another study, the top functions within the board circulated amongst 34 persons, mostly large producers.[62]

Table 5.11:   El Salvador: development of the domestic cotton market and
cotton production, 1950–85

Period	Production[a]	Consumption[b] (%)
1950–9	500.2	12.9
1960–9	1189.0	15.3
1970–9	1493.0	16.9
1980	997.3	26.2
1981	912.7	16.7
1982	885.1	25.8
1983	656.2	46.6
1984	658.7	43.8
1985	407.6	72.1

SOURCE: Harness and Pugh (1970) p. 16; Hernández (1980) p. 58; Comité
Consultivo Internacional del Algodón (1986); and sources listed in Annex 1.

NOTES: [a] '000 quintals ginned cotton.
    [b] Consumption on the local market as % of production.

COPAL buys unginned cotton offered by the growers, processes it,
classifies the cotton and sells both the ginned cotton and the by-
products (linter, seeds, and so on). There are four purchase-centres,
spread over the various cotton regions, which have a total of 12
desmotadoras. In order to sell the cotton on the local market COPAL
has a sales agreement with the textile industry. The quantity of cotton
that can be offered is fixed before the harvest at a price equal to that
of the cotton that will be exported. In this way the local textile
industry receives the cotton at more favourable prices than when it
had to buy cotton fibre on the world market, by saving costs involved
with the import of cotton fibre.

The sales on the home market fluctuated over the past 35 years and
increased in the 1960s and 1970s. In the 1950s these amounted to
nearly 65,000 quintals of ginned cotton on a yearly average, which
increased to 252,000 in the 1970s or nearly 17 per cent of the annual
production. In the 1980s its share has increased because of the falling
production of the past years, as is shown in Table 5.11. This Table
also indicates the development of a strong textile industry in El
Salvador during the past decades, which in 1978 employed almost
20,000 people.[63]

Although the internal cotton trade belongs to COPAL by law there
exists a certain margin for trade outside the cooperative, which is

shown by the operations of middlemen in local cotton trade. These are usually large, but also medium-sized, cotton producers who also provide credit facilities and often supply inputs, and at the same time lease out land to the potential cotton growers. In general, the small and medium-sized cotton producers work with the middlemen. Because of the long time-lag between the sowing of cotton seed and payment for the product delivered at COPAL (17 months), these producers, with poor financial resources, largely depend upon financiers other than COPAL or the banks. COPAL's lack of storage facilities, where large producers are treated more favourably, also forces small and medium-sized producers to sell to others who do have storage-room at COPAL at their disposal. Other producers are not members of COPAL because they do not meet the requirements, and thus are forced to sell their production to the middlemen too.[64]

The operations of middlemen are made possible because as producers they can apply for authorisation for larger areas of cotton than they really intend to cultivate. In this way they also receive credit facilities from the banks for a larger amount than they need for their own cotton area and use these loans for facilitating credits to other producers who deliver cotton to them.

Some evidence of this phenomenon in the 1970s can be found in the fact that many large cotton growers obtained yields far above what could be technically obtained in El Salvador at that time. Also field-research, carried out in 1986, showed that 30 per cent of cotton production was purchased from other growers.[65]

7. CONCLUSIONS

The introduction of cotton-growing formed part of a diversification of agricultural exports in Nicaragua and El Salvador in the 1950s and started from a different historical background in both countries. In Nicaragua in the nineteenth and the first part of the twentieth centuries, coffee principally played the role of capital accumulation without radically changing the dominant relations of production. Cotton production accelerated the capitalist development of Nicaragua, especially in the Pacific region, where it eliminated the production of basic grains, expelled subsistence farming to other regions and caused a process of proletarianisation in the countryside. In this country it was a new rural bourgeoisie, not associated directly with the Somoza clan nor with the traditional landed coffee oligarchy, who made the investments in cotton-growing.

In the past century and the first half of the present one, El Salvador was more integrated in the world market of primary products and capitalist development had advanced further in the countryside. The expansion of cotton-growing did not affect its economy as radically as in Nicaragua. On the other hand, the effects of the cotton expansion were more severe for the countryside in El Salvador, because of the incorporation of the last available land of the agricultural frontier. Unlike in Nicaragua, cotton farming in El Salvador had taken place since the 1920s based on a local textile industry, and it was the agro-export bourgeoisie which diversified its economic activities with investments in the cotton sector and soon formed an organisation to defend its interests.

The different origins of the bourgeoisies involved in cotton-growing for export – in El Salvador an agro-export bourgeoisie with an oligarchic character, in Nicaragua a newly formed bourgeoisie – has strongly influenced the production structure in the past decades, reflected in the tendency towards concentration in each country.

The sector showed signs of high concentration from the very beginning in El Salvador. This was noticed in the early 1950s, when very large producers already existed and continued to dominate production until the 1980s. This concentrated character is not only limited to the agrarian phase of the sector but is also found in the intermediary trading of cotton, the granting of private credit facilities, in the agro-industry and exports, in industry associated with the cotton sector and the trade of agricultural inputs.

Although the cotton bourgeoisie in Nicaragua did not have much presence in agro-industry nor in cotton commerce nor in financial activities, the sector became concentrated in the agrarian phase. This concentration mainly took place in the 1960s, which resulted in a similar degree of concentration in cotton production as in El Salvador. In both countries the small and medium-sized producers have had a significant role in production, although in El Salvador the small producers have had relatively more importance than in Nicaragua over the past two decades.

The structure of commerce in the countries provides an indication of the distribution of the surplus in the sphere of circulation of the cotton sector. In El Salvador export and internal trade is monopolised by COPAL and controlled by the agro-export bourgeoisie, while in Nicaragua before 1979 exports were in the hands of trading companies, mainly dominated by foreign capital and with an oligopolistic character. Outside COPAL's control in El Salvador, large cotton-growers operated as intermediary tradesmen, mostly for smaller producers, and also granted credit facilities, leased land and supplied inputs. For the agro-export bourgeoisie these activities guaranteed extra income in the form of land rents, interest and commercial profits. In Nicaragua the internal cotton trade had a more heterogeneous character. The ginning industry, middlemen and many export houses participated in the domestic cotton market. As in El Salvador, middlemen operated as financiers of production and were at the same time suppliers of agricultural inputs. The use of forward contracting, together with credit facilities turned out to be unfavourable in both countries for small and medium-sized producers, and enabled the trading agents to obtain large profits from the intermediate trade margins of cotton commerce and agricultural inputs, as well as high credit interests at the cost of the cotton producers.

Analysis of the sector in the 1980s shows remarkable changes in production structures, and in the case of Nicaragua also in the trade structure of cotton. Land reform programmes affected large cotton properties in both countries. In Nicaragua a state sector was formed which was principally based on the expropriation of large cotton farms owned by Somoza-related landlords covering a quarter of the total cotton area. A co-operative sector was also formed among the small producers. State farms and the co-operative sector increased their participation in the cotton sector to 50 per cent in recent years. Although the private sector of medium-sized and large producers is slowly decreasing, their participation in the cotton sector and their role in production remains important.

In El Salvador the land reform programme created a co-operative sector based on the expropriation of large estates which represented 27 per cent of the total cotton area and is now responsable for half of cotton production as a result of the declining area of private sector production. The continuing crisis in the cotton sector and the unfavourable position of the small producers has strongly reduced their role in the production.

Whereas in El Salvador nothing changed in the sphere of cotton trade, in Nicaragua nationalisation took place. This eliminated the formerly flourishing intermediary trade and the domination of foreign capital in cotton exports. It also assured state control of the foreign exchange generated. Here additional measures gave overall state control on the prices of agricultural inputs, of the processing of cotton and the producers' price for cotton.

It can be concluded that despite land reform in El Salvador there have been few basic changes in the distribution of economic surplus in the cotton sector. Although land reform did have some effect on land holdings, the role of the agro-export bourgeoisie in cotton trade, processing, loans, land leasing and services in the sector has been virtually untouched. It illustrates the limits of the reform programme that started in 1980.

For Nicaragua it can be concluded that changes in the production structure and trade have changed the distribution of economic surplus in favour of both the state and co-operative producers, at the expense of the agro-export bourgeoisie, middlemen and foreign capital who lost part of the production to the state and also the extra income from leasehold properties, commercial activities, exports, and so on. The total impact on small and medium-sized (non-co-operative) growers is still unclear. The participation of the state increased, because of state production, its monopoly in cotton marketing and far-reaching control over prices in the entire sector. However, the policy of incentives for cotton production has reduced the net flow of foreign exhange to the state.

Appendix 5.1:   El Salvador and Nicaragua: development of the cotton sector, 1950–85

Period/ harvest year[a]	El Salvador			Nicaragua		
	Area[b]	Production[c]	Yield[d]	Area[b]	Production[c]	Yield[d]
1950–4	36.6	261.7	7.2	63.6	410.2	6.4
1955–9	62.7	738.6	11.8	111.0	918.4	8.3
1960–4	128.1	1433.6	11.2	135.8	1643.0	12.1
1965–9	79.7	944.4	11.8	192.0	1986.1	10.3
1970–4	115.2	1488.0	12.9	203.4	2418.1	11.9
1975–9	125.5	1498.1	11.9	222.1	2113.3	9.5
1980–1	83.1	997.3	12.0	134.7	1645.8	12.2
1981–2	82.8	912.7	11.0	132.7	1387.4	10.5
1982–3	71.3	885.1	12.4	129.2	1753.2	13.6
1983–4	54.4	656.2	12.1	167.6	1884.5	11.2
1984–5	53.5	658.7	12.3	159.0	1505.6	9.5
1985–6	39.3	407.6	10.4	125.0	1106.3	8.9

SOURCE: Hernández (1980) p. 26; COPAL, *Memorias*, various years; Arias (1984) p. 32; Banco Central de Nicaragua (1978a) p. 73; Evans (1987); Stevenson (1963); Harness and Pugh (1970).

NOTES: [a] All data calculated as annual averages.
        [b] '000 manzanas.
        [c] '000 quintals ginned cotton.
        [d] Quintals ginned cotton/manzana.

Notes

1. The author is Research Fellow at the Faculty of Economics and the Development Research Institute at the University of Tilburg (The Netherlands). The research for this article was made possible partly by the Centre for Study and Documentation on Latin America (CEDLA) in Amsterdam.
2. Williams (1986) p. 13.
3. Biderman (1983) p. 13.
4. Vilas (1984) p. 77.
5. Biderman (1983) p. 13.
6. Wheelock (1980) pp. 142–56. Herrera Zúñiga (1980) also analysed these economic groups, their pacts and conflicts between BANIC, BAN-AMERICA and the dominating group around Somoza.
7. Núñez (1980) p. 29.
8. Vilas (1984) pp. 77–8.
9. De Franco and Hurtado de Vijil (1978) pp. 44–5.
10. Pelupessy (1984) pp. 21–2.
11. Browning (1975) pp. 345–8.
12. See, for example, Sebastian (1986) pp. 32–5; and Baloyra (1986) pp. 41–51.
13. Browning, (1975) pp. 354–7.
14. In Annex 1 a résumé of the data used in this section is given. The sources for the Figures are also found there.
15. Navas (1983) pp. 7–10.
16. Baumeister *et al.* (1983) pp. 65–6. Credit facilities for individual producers were conditional on obtaining a minimum yield of 25 quintals of unginned cotton per manzana in the previous year.
17. Baumeister (1985) p. 58.
18. In 1963 the cotton area was 134,700 manzanas.
19. Baumeister *et al.* (1983) pp. 50–8. For example, in harvest year 1964–5 more than half of the cotton area of producers with less than 50 manzanas was rented, unlike the large producers (over 500 manzanas), who only rented a third of the acreage cultivated with cotton.
20. In the 1970s it was mostly the producers with over 1,000 manzanas of cotton area who produced the crop on rented land (75 per cent). For all growers this was 55 per cent, mainly for fiscal motives and to obtain more bank loans.
21. 76 per cent of the requested loans of medium-sized producers were financed by the banks (1973). For large producers this was 95 per cent, while for the small ones it was only 32 per cent.
22. Known under decree numbers 3 and 38 of 20 July and 8 August 1979.
23. Data from MIDINRA.
24. Thome and Kaimowitz (1985) p. 300.
25. In the Pacific region; in other regions respectively 1,000 and 100 manzanas. For an evaluation of Nicaraguan land reforms see, for example, Deere, Marchetti and Reinhardt (1985) p. 77 *et seq*.
26. Baumeister *et al.* (1983) p. 74. During the period from 1978 until 1981

the share of cotton production on land in property in the region of León increased from 41.6 per cent to 57.8 per cent.

27. Baumeister *et al.* (1983) p. 85.
28. Evans (1987) p. 12.
29. Colburn (1986) p. 55.
30. The data which can be found for harvest years 1980–1 and 1981–2 is rare and appears to be unreliable. The data presented for 1983–4 and 1984–5 is more reliable and has been confirmed by field research in the region for the co-operative development Petacaltepe, located in the province of Chinandega. Here small private producers obtained a yield of 33 quintals per manzana, the CAS 20 quintals, the CCS 22 quintals and the medium-sized and large producers an average yield of 39 quintals of unginned cotton per manzana in harvest year 1983–4. The total area which was investigated amounted to 7,000 manzanas (Vermeer (1986) pp. 55, 68, 74, 81).
31. Ibid., p. 68.
32. For 1983–4 it was estimated that a minimum production of 30 quintals per manzana was needed for production without loss. In 1984–5 the condition for the co-operatives to obtain agricultural credits was having obtained a yield of 20 quintals of unginned cotton per manzana the year before.
33. Evans (1987) p. 24.
34. Data used from Colindres (1977) p. 73, and CEPAL (1971) p. 94. Here small producers have a size of less than 15 manzanas. Large producers have an acreage of more than 140 manzanas.
35. Browning (1975), p. 371.
36. Arias (1984) p. 27. The potential acreage appropriate for cotton cultivation was estimated at 100,000 manzanas.
37. Smaller than 20 manzanas in this case. Browning (1975) p. 371.
38. With a size between 20 and 100 manzanas.
39. For 1978 Arias (1984, p. 59) gives a list of 41 cotton growers who produced more than 10,000 quintals of unginned cotton and so dominated 18 per cent of total annual production. The largest producers, the Dueñas, obtained at that time an output of 69,000 quintals of unginned cotton, Wright 34,000 and Kriete 21,000 quintals.
40. Williams (1986) p. 32.
41. Hernández (1980) p. 47. The technically maximum possible yield per manzana is about 40 quintals of unginned cotton.
42. Larger farms (>500 mzs) rented 32 per cent of their land, while medium-sized and small growers rented 68 per cent (Arias (1984) p. 29).
43. In harvest year 1969–70 24 per cent of small producers financed their cotton production by other means than bank loans, unlike the medium-sized and large cotton growers, 11 per cent of whom used other means. In 1974–5 this was 27 per cent and 5 per cent. (Arias (1984) pp. 68–9).
44. Hernández (1980) pp. 40–1.
45. Pelupessy (1987) p. 227.
46. An evaluation of the land reform programme can be found in ibid.
47. Reinhardt (1987) pp. 944–5.
48. MAG (1983) pp. 11–22; field research of 1986.

49. For example, by 1982–3 it was reported that 49.6 per cent of the cotton acreage was leasehold property (MAG (1983) p. 34). Field research carried out in 1986 also showed that more than half the cotton production took place on rented land.
50. During field research (1985–6) carried out in the main cotton area of the provinces of Usulután, La Paz, San Miguel and San Vicente it was impossible to find a cotton producer of a size less than 26 manzanas.
51. The figures given are for 1969–70 and did not change significantly in the 1970s.
52. CONAL (1973) p. 62.
53. CONAL was set up in 1966.
54. Núñez (1980) p. 46.
55. Ibid., p. 47.
56. See, for example, Cruz and Hoadley (1975) p. 10.
57. Evans (1987) Appendixes 12 and 13.
58. CEPAL (1985) p. 101.
59. During the period 1980–5, the guaranteed cotton price increased from 790 *cordobas* to 9650 *cordobas* a quintal of ginned cotton.
60. Méndez (1982) pp. 624–7.
61. Data from Colindres (1977) p. 55 and Appendix 67.
62. Arias (1984) pp. 104–7.
63. Ibid., p. 181.
64. Hernández (1980) pp. 40–2.
65. Data from an unpublished study of the Development Research Institute, Tilburg.

Bibliography

Arias, Salvador (1988) Los Subsistemas de Agro Exportación en El Salvador (San Salvador: UCA Editores).
Baloyra, E. (1986), *El Salvador en Transición* (San Salvador: UCA Editores).
Banco Central de Nicaragua (1977), *Encuesta Sobre las Perspectivas de la Actividad Algodonera en Nicaragua* (Managua: Banco Central de Nicaragua).
—— (1978a), *Indicadores Económicos* (Managua: Banco Central de Nicaragua).
—— (1978b), *Informe Anual, 1977* (Managua: Banco Central de Nicaragua).
—— (1979), *Informe Anual, 1978* (Managua: Banco Central de Nicaragua).
Baumeister, Eduardo (1985), 'Agrarian Reform in Nicaragua', in R. Harris and C. M. Vilas (eds), *Nicaragua: A Revolution under Siege* (London: Zed Books).
Baumeister, Eduardo *et al.* (1983), *El Subsistema del Algodón en Nicaragua* (Managua: INIES/CRIES).
Biderman, Jaime (1983), 'The Development of Capitalism in Nicaragua: a Political Economic History', in *Latin American Perspectives*, vol. 10, no. 36 (Winter 1983) pp. 7–32.

Browning, D. (1971), *Landscape and Society* (Oxford: Oxford University Press).

CEPAL (Comision Económica Para America Latina) (1971), *El Salvador, Características Generales de la Utilización y Distribución de la Tierra* (Mexico: CEPAL).

—— (1985), *America Latina y la Economía Mundial del Algodón* (Santiago de Chile: CEPAL).

CEPAL/FAO/OIT (1980), *Tenencia de la Tierra y Desarrollo Rural en Centroamérica* (San José: EDUCA).

Colburn, Forrest D. (1986), *Post-Revolutionary Nicaragua, State, Class and the Dilemmas of Agrarian Policy* (Berkeley: University of California Press).

Colindres, E. (1977), *Fundamentos Económicos de la Burguesia Salvadoreña* (San Salvador: UCA Editores).

Comité Consultivo Internacional del Algodón (1986), *Algodón: Estadisticas Mundiales*, vol. 39, no. 4 (April).

CONAL (Comisión Nacional del Algodón) (1973), *Informe 1971/72* (Managua: CONAL).

COPAL (Cooperativa Algodonera Salvadoreña) (1985), *Memoria Cosecha 1984/85* (San Salvador: COPAL).

—— (1986), *Memoria Cosecha 1985/86* (San Salvador: COPAL).

—— (1987), *Memoria Cosecha 1986/87* (San Salvador: COPAL).

Cruz, Ernesto and Hoadley, Kenneth L. (1975), 'The Effect of Government Trade Policy on Private Sector Exports: the Case of Nicaraguan Cotton', in IDB, *Proceedings of the Seminar on Agricultural Policy: A Limiting Factor in the Development Process* (Washington, D.C.).

Deere, Carmen D., Marchetti, Peter and Reinhardt, Nola (1985), 'The Peasant and the Development of Sandinista Agrarian Policy', *Latin American Research Review*, vol. XX, no. 3, pp. 75–109.

De Franco, Maria A. and Hurtado de Vijil, Maria (1978), 'Algunos Aspectos del Funcionamiento Socio-Económico de Nicaragua', in *Pensamiento Centroamericano*, no. 159, pp. 38–54.

Dirección General de Estadísticas y Censo (1961), *Resumen Estadístico, 1950–1960* (Managua: DGEC).

Evans, Trevor (1987), *El Algodón: Un Cultivo en Debate* (Managua: CRIES).

FUSADES (1984), *La Reactivación del Cultivo de Algodón* (San Salvador: FUSADES).

Harness, Vernon L. and Pugh, Robert D. (1970), *Cotton in Central America* (Washington, D.C.: US Department of Agriculture).

Hernández Cuellar, Gracia M. and Amaya Serrano, Rhina A. (1980), *Mecanismos para la Comercialización Interna y Externa del Algodón*, Facultad de Ciencias Económicas, Universidad Centroamericana, San Salvador (unpublished thesis).

Herrero Zúniga, René (1980), 'Nicaragua: el Desarrollo Capitalista Dependiente y la Crisis de la Dominación Burguesa, 1950–1980', in *Centroamérica en Crisis* (Mexico: Centro de Estudios Internacionales).

ISTA (Instituto Salvadoreña de Transformación Agraria) (1985), *El Cultivo del Algodón, Areas y Producciones en el Sector Reformado durante el periodo 1980–1984* (San Salvador: Ministerio de Agricultura y Ganaderia).

López, José Roberto (1986), 'La Nacionalización del Comercio Exterior en El Salvador: Mitos y Realidades en Torno al Café', in *Estudios Centroamericanos*, nos 451–2 (May–June) pp. 389–410.

MAG (Ministerio de Agricultura y Ganadería) (1983), *Evaluación del Cultivo del Algodón cosecha 1982/83* (San Salvador: Ministerio de Agricultura y Ganaderia).

Méndez, Ana M. (1983), *Incidencias de la Producción Algodonera en las Políticas del Estado de El Salvador (período 1940–1980)*, (San Salvador: Facultad de Ciencias Económicas, Universidad Centroamericana).

Navas Mendoza, A. (1983), *Algunos Elementos para un Análisis de los Periodos Críticos del Algodón en Nicaragua* (León: UNAN).

Núñez Soto, Orlando (1980), *El Somocismo y el Modelo Capitalista Agroexportadora* (Managua: Depto. de Ciencias Sociales, UNAN).

OEDEC (1975), *Compendio Estadístico, 1965–1974* (Managua: OEDEC).

Pelupessy, Wim (1984), *El Sector Agroexportador de El Salvador* (Tilburg: Katholieke Universiteit Brabant).

—— (1987), 'Reforma Agraria y Sector Agroexportador en El Salvador', in *Estudios Centroamericanos*, vol. XLII, no. 461 (March) pp. 227–36.

Reinhardt, Nola (1987), 'Agro-exports and the Peasantry in the Agrarian Reforms of El Salvador and Nicaragua', in *World Development*, vol. 15, no. 7, pp. 941–59.

Sebastian, Luis de (1986), 'Consideraciones Político-Económicas Sobre la Oligarquía en El Salvador', in *El Salvador, Estado Oligarquico y Desarrollo Económico-Social, 1945–1979* (México: CINAS) pp. 29–48.

Stevenson, Joseph H. (1963), *Cotton Production in Central America* (Washington, D.C.: US Department of Agriculture).

Thome, J. R. and Kaimowitz, D. (1985), 'Nicaragua's Agrarian Reform: the First Year (1979–80)', in T. W. Walker (ed.), *Nicaragua en Revolution* (New York: Praeger).

Vermeer, Riné (1986), *Landbouwcoöperaties in Nicaragua* (Tilburg: Instituut voor Ontwikkelingsvraagstukken).

Vilas, C. M. (1984), *Perfiles de la Revolución Sandinista* (Havana).

Warnken, P. F. (1975) *The Agricultural Development of Nicaragua* (Columbia: University of Missouri Press).

Wheelock R. Jaime (1980), *Imperialismo y Dictadura* (Mexico City: Siglo Veintiuno).

Williams, Robert G. (1986) *Export Agriculture and the Crisis in Central America* (Chapel Hill, N. C. and London: University of North Carolina Press).

6 Developments in the Coffee and Cotton Sectors of El Salvador and Perspectives for Agrarian Policy in the 1980s

Wim Pelupessy

1. INTRODUCTION

The crisis of the 1980s appears to be questioning the basic viability of the agro-export development model in Central America. The effects of slackening world market demand, unstable international prices, worsening terms of trade and negative net external capital flows have combined with those of social unrest, repression and in most countries even civil war, resulting in serious external and internal imbalances of the overall economic system. Some studies speak of the end of an era, the consequences of which might be comparable to those of the disappearance of the international indigo markets in the nineteenth century. Then, the inability to make profits on the world market resulted in a drastic change in the production structure of Central America.[1]

In this chapter attention will be paid to what may be called the supply side of the export economy and the way this has been influenced by changes in the external environment. Even before the recent crisis, the structure of the postwar development of the region was described by the Economic Commission of Latin America (ECLA) as superimposed, externally determined and of an exclusive nature.[2] Another longer-term study pointed more explicitly to a probable breakdown of social and economic relations as a consequence of oligarchic-based agricultural export growth.[3] It seems that historically the impact of export growth on the balance of payments of the countries, on government revenues, total value-added, domestic savings and on the financial sector has been insufficient to generate a balanced and autonomous development. The economic structure is such that the movements in the agro-export sector determine the aggregate demand of the countries and above all their capacity to import. That has made trade among the Central American countries, even of industrial products, very sensitive to price movements and world demand for primary agricultural commodities, especially coffee.[4] The creation of the Central American Common Market increased interdependence, but also integrated economic dependence on external factors.[5] The margin for any countercyclical economic policy of the governments concerned is very limited. The previously mentioned ECLA report emphasised the need to design an alternative strategy for the region, directed at structural change. However, a recent exhaustive review of existing empirical work in this field pointed out that to reach relevant results for policy-making, research must be done in detail, analysing the export patterns at sectorial levels of specific countries.[6] Another recent publication stated: 'Although the decisive importance of sectoral considerations in adjustment has been stressed by some authors, there has been very limited research on countries' sectoral responses to changes in the international environment and their links with overall macroeconomic adjustment.'[7]

In this chapter we shall present some results of research in this direction for El Salvador. In El Salvador, production conditions in the agro-export sectors changed drastically during the 1980s because of the economic crisis, civil war and the application of agrarian and other reforms.

The macroeconomic importance of those export sectors has not been reduced. The first three export products, coffee, cotton and sugar, counted for 68 per cent of the export value of goods at the beginning of the 1980s and for about 75 per cent during the two years 1986–8, while the export tax on coffee fluctuates between a fifth and a third of total tax income. However, the situation calls for a revision of agrarian policy based on a reorientation of the role of these sectors in the economy. In analysing the case of two of the most important traditional agricultural export products, we shall also consider the impact of the new role of the state in their production and commercialisation. Attention will focus on the main factors which have affected profitability, the relative position of different types of producers and conditions for accumulation in rural areas of El Salvador.

In this study, use has been made of both published and unpublished material obtained from recent fieldwork done by the Development Research Institute (IVO) in El Salvador. In the conclusion we shall attempt some recommendations for agrarian policy and generalise some of the arguments of the Salvadorean case to the rest of Central America.

2.   CHANGES IN A TRADITIONAL AGRO-EXPORT MODEL

The introduction of structural reforms in 1980 was intended to make possible far-reaching state intervention in the productive, commercial and financial spheres of key sectors of the economy, in order to influence significantly the generation and distribution of overall surplus. The agrarian reform, the nationalisation of banking and of the export trade of coffee and sugar and the regulation of the internal commerce of basic grains, form part of an overall strategy to reactivate and change the stagnating accumulation model of the 1970s. It is perhaps in El Salvador that one can trace more clearly than in any other country of the region the consequences of what the Economic Commission of Latin America has called 'the superimposed development model'. Unparalleled economic growth in the postwar era has been accompanied by a rigidly biased agro-export production structure, increasing external dependency, the virtual absence of redistribution of the results of this growth, especially in the rural areas, resulting in a stagnating internal market. This led to a generalised economic, social and political crisis, in which an armed challenge to traditional power emerged at the beginning of the 1980s.[8]

The reforms were necessary for both the implementation of a new (counterrevolutionary) sociopolitical model as well as for what the policy makers later called a 'social market economy', in which the state must exercise a fundamental role in the orientation and development of the internal market, in which different kinds of producers are going to participate.[9]

The agrarian reform is intended to play a fundamental role in the modernisation of the productive system and in the efforts to attain a more balanced growth. This means that 'the reform must be concerned with the ownership of land and capital and at the same time . . . must produce a system of land tenure that is capable of achieving sustainable increases in crop production – for export and domestic needs – through an intensified and efficient use of a limited resource base.'[10]

Although we shall concentrate on the impact of seven years of implementation of this and the other reforms in two of the most important traditional agricultural export sectors, it will be impossible to leave aside what has happened to the other sectors, even outside agriculture. The spread of ownership of the means of production and of the interests of the agro-export-based Salvadorean oligarchy is of such a generalised nature that one must at least consider the development of the relationship between the agro-export and other sectors.[11]

3. AGRARIAN REFORM

There have until now been two types of land expropriation under the agrarian reform. The so-called phase I, affected landholdings in excess of 500 hectares. The Salvadorean Agrarian Transformation Institute (ISTA), set up in 1976, intervened in 471 properties in 1980, forming 314 new agrarian production co-operatives with the permanent workers who were present on the estate at the moment of expropriation. Each co-operative had to have a minimum of 25 members and the management had to operate under ISTA direction.

The previous owners were compensated by ISTA in cash and (redeemable) bonds and do have the right to claim, depending on the quality, 100 to 150 hectares of the affected land. It is estimated that the total area of these claims will amount to 6 per cent of the phase I affected land. More or less the same quantity of land from the co-operatives is also claimed by the state as national reservation land. About half of the newly formed co-operatives have areas of more than 500 hectares and the other half have smaller extensions of land. Most of the properties have a significant part of their land assigned to export crops and cattle-raising. However, in many cases the previous owner was able to separate the related coffee processing plant from the agrarian property and in this way prevented its expropriation. Only seven of the smaller coffee plants, representing together less than 5 per cent of the installed coffee processing capacity of the country, were affected by the reform. One year after the introduction of the reform, it was decided to give traditional agrarian co-operatives established in the 1970s the same treatment under ISTA control as those set up under phase I.

Table 6.1:   Agrarian structure, 1985

Category	Extension agricultural land Area ('000 ha.)		Percentage		Population '000	%
Phase I						
New co-operatives	214	Export crops 49	15	Export 23		
		Basic grains 34		Basic 16		
		Rest 131		Rest 61	145	8
Trad. co-operatives[a]	57		4			
Phase III						
New smallholders	97	Export crops –	7	Export –		
	(62)	Basic grains 89	(4)	Basic 92	382	21
		Rest 7		Rest 8	(270)	(15)
Total reformed area	368		26		527	29
	(333)		(23)		(415)	(23)
Non-reformed area	1093	Export crops 195	74	Export 18	1304	71
	(1128)	Basic grains 299	(77)	Basic 27	(1416)	(77)
		Rest 599		Rest 55		
Total agric. land in exploitation	1461		100		1831	100

SOURCE: Ministerio de Agricultura y Ganadería (1985), *V Evaluación del Proceso de la Reforma Agraria* (San Salvador).

NOTES: Export crops: Coffee, cotton, sugar cane. Basic grains: Corn, beans, sorghum and rice; Rest: Pastures, forests, other cultivated products, fallow land, etc.
Figures in brackets indicate an estimate of phase III land/beneficiaries discounting properties left out of the programme in 1986 (extension smaller than 7 ha.).
[a] Supposedly basic-grains growers.

Another type of land expropriation which has been implemented was called phase III or 'land to the tiller', where small tenant farmers could claim land to a maximum of 7 hectares from owners who own less than 100 hectares. This limit was introduced to exclude from the reform much of the land lease system of the large cotton and sugar cane growers. In 1987 approximately a third of cotton land was still rented and when we exclude the co-operatives of phase I, it appears that more than 60 per cent of the private cotton areas are rented. The small tenants, mostly basic grain growers, can ask the National Land Financing Agency (FINATA) to buy the land from its former owners and to sell it to them on a lease with a 30-year period to amortise the costs. During this period the new smallholder is not allowed to sell or lease the land. Until the end of December 1985 there were about 9,000 properties affected and 64,000 claims, but half of these properties were themselves smaller than 7 hectares. It is probable that these small properties will be excluded from phase III.[12]

Table 6.1 gives the new agrarian structure after six years of agrarian reform implementation, also taking into consideration the land area dedicated to the cultivation of export crops and basic grains. The reformed area, taking the two phases together, amounts to 26 per cent of total agricultural land in exploitation and benefits 29 per cent of the agricultural population. If the smaller properties of phase III are excluded, these proportions will reduce to 23 per cent each. The total population estimate takes account of the effects of the war (victims) and associated migratory movements of refugees and displaced persons out of the rural areas. Since about 1986 a small but continuing stream of peasant population has returned to the countryside, but it is almost impossible to make reliable estimates of the effects of this.

It will be clear from the information in the Table that a significant part of the area (23 per cent) of the new phase I co-operative sector, is dedicated to the export crops of coffee, cotton and sugar cane, compared to 18 per cent in the non-reformed sector. Approximately 90 per cent of the coffee land, 65 per cent of the cotton and 60 per cent of the sugar cane areas still belong to the latter sector. Over two thirds of the 16 per cent of the co-operative land dedicated to the cultivation of basic grains is worked on individual family plots and only one-third on collective land. A recent USAID investigation showed that members of the newly formed co-operatives even consider the assigning of the individual plots of land, which enable them to grow the needed food crops, as the main, and in some cases the only, benefit of reform.[13]

It is also notorious that the percentage of reserved land (mainly pastures, fallow lands and forests) is slightly higher in the new co-operatives than in the non-reformed sector. This is partly a consequence of the way the former owners and landlords used to manage agricultural activity in El Salvador. In phase III smallholders should have received 7 per cent of the agricultural land, benefiting 21 per cent of the agricultural population, giving an average of 1.5 ha. for each family. But the previously mentioned exclusion proposed in 1986 of potentially expropriated land lowers this average to 1.3 ha. The average landholding area for the new smallholders is well below what a family may require to survive in agriculture.[14] Only about 6 per cent of these smallholders are at present organised in co-operatives. When one compares the man–land ratios of the different

Table 6.2:   Index of crop earning capacity, 1971–85 (value-added/ha.)
Corn = 100

Crop		1971	1980	1985
Export crops:	Coffee	1032	1787	939
	Cotton	523	392	407
	Sugar cane	675	703	493
Basic grains:	Corn	100	100	100
	Beans	200	156	64
	Sorghum	99	64	54
	Rice	532	446	326

SOURCE: Banco Central de Reserva de El Salvador (1986), *Revista Oct.–Dec.*, p. 97; Ministerio de Planificación (1984), *Indicadores Enero–Dic.*, p. 33; Ruíz, S. (1979), 'Modernización Agrícola en El Salvador', *Estudios Sociales Centroamericanos*, no. 22 (Jan.–April) p. 75.

land tenure sectors, the proportion in phase III is about three times as high as the average in the non-reformed sector and eight times that of phase I properties.

The stronger agro-export orientation of phase I co-operatives is another advantage of this sector, bearing in mind that earning capacity of these crops is much higher than that of basic grains.

The information in Table 6.2 shows that in 1985, as a result of productivity and price effects, value-added per hectare of sugar cane and cotton was more than four times that of corn, and for coffee it was more than nine times the rate for basic grains. Rice seems to be the exception in the basic grains group. The degree of modernisation of the crop is one of the factors which can explain these differences. More than 40 per cent of the area dedicated to export crops can, on average, be classified as modernised and almost 15 per cent (mainly coffee) as non-modernised, while these proportions are reversed for basic grains.[15] The percentage of entrepreneurial return in value-added for export crops is also, on average, more than four times that for basic grains (again rice is the exception).[16]

A third type of land expropriation which was included in the original land reform programme but has not yet been implemented is the so-called phase II of the agrarian reform. This was to include properties larger than 150 and smaller than 500 hectares, including the majority of the coffee estates belonging to large producers. The execution of this phase was announced in December 1987 and generated a lot of uncertainty and protests among large landowners and, at the same time, expectations and demands from workers and peasant organisations, both those pro-government and those in opposition. However, the new Constitution of 1983 excluded properties of less than 245 hectares from this reform, so that the original land area which would have been affected under phase II decreased from 24 per cent of national agricultural land to an insignificant 3 per cent.[17]

When we compare the number of beneficiaries of the first and third phases of land reform with the number of potential beneficiaries in the agricultural population there are two relevant groups: permanent workers and small tenant-farmers. A rough estimate based on 1985 data gives a figure of 328,000 families in the agricultural sector, of which approximately 27 per cent had tenant status and 23 per cent were permanent workers.[18] Phase I beneficiaries are therefore about a third of the potential beneficiaries and those of phase III about 40 per cent.[19] The majority of the agrarian families (semi-proletarians, small peasants and temporary wage-earners) remain outside the reform (see also the percentages in Table 6.1).

On the other hand, the reform has also had its effects on the non-reformed part of agriculture. There is, for instance, the resulting uncertainty regarding the precise limits of the reform. This has led to the division of some large landed properties, either by selling parts, distributing to family members or nominating figureheads as owners. Today, it is difficult to find private estates larger than 245 hectares in El Salvador, even in the agro-export sectors. In the more detailed treatment of the export crops we shall also deal with the consequences of the complementary banking and export trade reforms. But first, it is useful to have a brief look at the functioning of the newly formed co-operative sector.

4. THE CO-OPERATIVE SECTOR

Table 6.3 presents the evolution of the cultivated and collectively worked areas of 99 coffee, 66 cotton and 120 sugar cane co-operatives. The total area dedicated to export crops did not show significant changes. The cotton area declined, mainly due to war and world market conditions, but that of sugar cane increased by almost the same number of hectares, due to favourable economic results.

The collectively worked basic grains area has diminished to almost a third of its original size. Work on individual family plots and also

Table 6.3:   Collective land of co-operatives of agrarian reform
phase I (ha.)

Crops	1980–1	1981–2	1982–3	1983–4	1984–5
Coffee	21,795	18,992	19,320	18,944	19,682
Cotton	19,612	19,095	16,154	13,607	13,499
Sugarcane	10,618	11,006	12,793	13,906	15,910
Total export crops	52,025	49,093	48,267	46,457	49,091
Basic grains	29,063	27,359	16,222	13,010	9,780
Other crops	10,273	10,001	10,192	11,690	14,043
Total	91,361	86,453	74,681	71,157	72,914

SOURCE: MAG (1985), *V Evaluación del Proceso de la Reforma Agraria El Salvador*, December.

probably the effect of war conditions on co-operatives in the conflict areas of the country may have been responsible for this reduction, which has resulted in a 20 per cent decrease in the overall collective area. About 30 phase I co-operatives with a total extension of 15,000 ha. (7 per cent of the total co-operative area) have been abandoned because of the internal violence.[20]

The co-operatives also have other serious problems. In the financial sphere we can mention the accumulated debts: agrarian reform debt, emergency debt of 1980 provided by ISTA and the Agrarian Development Bank (BFA) to pay for other loans, and so on.[21] Another problem has been the delay of the marketing agencies for coffee (INCAFE, government) and cotton (COPAL, private) in handling the sale of the harvest. This delay, which in the case of coffee can be as much as 26 months, is causing serious financial problems to the majority of the co-operatives.

There are many complaints concerning the provision of credits to this sector, 85 per cent of which are destined for export crops. Unlike the first period of their existence, the co-operatives have subsequently made a profit.[22] However, these profits are mostly taken away by the banks to repay the above-mentioned debts. Although a significant number of co-operative members consider that their economic situation now is better than before the reform, it has to be noted that (hidden) unemployment among them is still high (at least 40 per cent), wages are low and members generally do not consider themselves as belonging to a co-operative, but still think in terms of the

Table 6.4:   Composition of agricultural value-added, 1980–5

Crops	1980	1981	1982	1983	1984	1985
Current prices						
Coffee	70.2	64.2	63.8	56.5	58.1	62.0
Cotton	7.5	7.0	5.2	6.7	5.6	5.9
Sugar cane	4.0	5.4	6.3	8.2	8.3	7.6
Basic grains	11.0	13.6	14.4	18.1	19.5	15.2
Other[a]	7.3	9.8	10.3	10.5	8.5	9.3
Total agric.	100	100	100	100	100	100
% Agric./Nat. V.A.	(27.8)	(24.2)	(23.2)	(21.3)	(19.9)	(18.2)
Constant prices:						
Coffee	50.3	50.7	53.1	49.3	46.8	48.0
Cotton	11.6	8.8	8.4	9.0	6.9	5.6
Sugar cane	3.8	3.5	3.9	5.3	5.8	6.2
Basic grains	22.1	22.5	20.0	22.4	26.6	25.6
Other[a]	12.2	14.6	14.6	14.0	13.9	14.6
Total agric.	100	100	100	100	100	100
% Agric./Nat. V.A.	(25.6)	(26.1)	(26.4)	(25.3)	(25.6)	(24.8)

SOURCE: BCR (1986), *Revista* (Oct.–Dec.) pp. 95, 97, 102, 103.

NOTES: [a] Other crops, cattlebreeding, forestry, fishery and poultry. Nat. V.A.: National value-added.

hacienda where they must try to get a family plot of land.[23] A recent case study has concluded that strong internal conflicts among members related to economic problems, frequent changes in membership, lack of participation in the internal organisation and the contradiction of individual versus collective work are major obstacles to the stability of the new co-operatives.[24] While a considerable part of the permanent labour (of members) is dedicated to low-productivity activities on the individual family plots, the co-operatives are inclined to contract more temporary and poorly remunerated outside labour for work on the collective areas.

5.   FACTORS AFFECTING EARNING CAPACITY

In the 1980s agriculture has decreased its participation in the national gross internal product at current prices, but has maintained its share in constant prices (see Table 6.4). Looking at the production structure of this sector, one can observe that coffee and cotton are responsible for the decline in monetary terms, together representing 78 per cent of the agricultural value-added in 1980 and 68 per cent in 1985. In real terms coffee has lost only a small fraction in this period, while cotton lost more than half of its initial weight. Sugar cane and basic grains increased their participation in real as well as monetary terms.

It is obvious that the evolution of world market prices has a direct impact on the current price values of coffee and cotton and in this way on their earning capacity. But there are other factors as well. Since 1979 there has been a constant decline in the cultivated area of cotton, irrespective of international price movements. Private, public and international development agencies have indicated which factors in their opinion have caused the main problems in the production of the two sectors during the 1980s.[25] Basically one can distinguish two types of problem, one which has directly affected profitability and the other related to the general climate of confidence of producers.

A first macroeconomic problem mentioned was the maintenance of an overvalued exchange rate, which has been a generalised practice in all the countries of Central America.[26] The authorities waited till 1986 to devalue the Salvadorean *colon* by 100 per cent, after parallel foreign-exchange markets had been in operation for some years. It has yet to be seen if the new fixed rate is the appropriate one. At the end of 1989 a further devaluation was expected for the coming year, as the black-market price of the *colon* was already 30 per cent above the official exchange rate.

Another problem is that producers consider the prices paid to them by INCAFE and COPAL respectively are too low. In the case of cotton, a stabilisation fund has existed since crop year 1983–4 which must ensure that producers receive a minimum price to cover their costs. One has to bear in mind that individual costs can deviate considerably from the average used by COPAL. The same argument can be used for the uniform prices paid to coffee growers. The delays of INCAFE and COPAL in handling sales have already been mentioned. Incompetence and inexperience in international marketing on the part of both the government functionaries of INCAFE and the private directors of the co-operative COPAL (all ten directors are cotton growers) seem to be among the reasons for these delays which raised the interest costs for the growers. The claim from the large coffee-growers that they might market their own coffee abroad better must therefore be seen mainly as political, as is their belief that in the period before the foundation of INCAFE the marketing was done more efficiently. This state agency inherited huge accumulated financial debts from its privately managed predecessor.[27] Two factors which reduce the surplus appropriation capacity of producers are the export taxes for coffee and the accumulated debts for both crops. A large indebtedness stems principally from working capital credits of past crop years combined with losses.

Among the problems mentioned which have had a direct impact on production costs are the increase in imported input prices, the higher costs for combating diseases and pests which have spread to considerable parts of the cultivated areas, and guerrilla activity which has principally affected the cotton sector. Other cost-increasing factors are the high nominal interest rates (13 to 15 per cent) and legal harvesting wages.

A second type of problem that has affected the confidence of producers has resulted in partial neglect and abandonment of cultivated areas, and the reduction of productivity, infrastructural investments and cultivation activities. Among the principal negative factors are mentioned the ongoing civil war, agrarian reform, nationalisation of coffee exports, the role of INCAFE and agrarian policy in general. To evaluate the effects of both types of factor we present the evolution of productive capacity of both sectors in their agricultural phase.

From Table 6.5 we deduce that in six years the coffee area declined by about 20 per cent, while the cotton area diminished dramatically by more than 50 per cent. This reduction becomes 80 per cent for the harvested area in crop year 1986–7 which occupied a total of only 12,600 hectares (also due to very unfavourable climatic conditions). Meanwhile, the real extent of the coffee area is overestimated because of partial abandonment and/or reduction of cultivation activities due to profitability problems and the war. By the late 1980s it was estimated that on average 46.6 per cent of the coffee area had not been worked properly, and in the conflict zones this percentage could be around 60 or 70 per cent.[28] Another problem is the coffee rust disease (*roya*), which has spread from the departments of San Miguel and Usulutan to almost the whole national coffee area. Only 40 per cent of the affected crops are treated and cultivators have tended to reduce the area treated.[29] The same tendency can be observed with other diseases and pests, both in the coffee and cotton sectors. Average yield of coffee during the 1980s has fluctuated for these reasons, and the levels are well below the 28.6 quintals per hectare considered as average for a 'medium efficient' producer in El Salvador.

Table 6.5:   Evolution of productive capacity, 1980–6

Crop year	Coffee (total)			Cotton (total)		
	Area ('000 ha.)	Yield[a] (qq/ha.)	Reformed sector in prod. (%)	Area ('000 ha.)	Yield[b] (qq/ha.)	Reformed sector in prod. (%)
1980–1	207.0	18.6	10.5	58.2	44.7	29.8
1981–2	207.0	18.4	11.6	52.4	41.4	37.4
1982–3	177.6	21.3	13.9	49.9	46.3	33.8
1983–4	173.7	16.6	12.6	38.1	44.4	38.6
1984–5	170.6	20.9	14.1	37.5	45.1	41.9
1985–6	163.6	15.7	13.3	27.5	37.7	44.7

SOURCE: MAG (1985), *V Evaluación del Proceso de la Reforma Agraria* (San Salvador) p. 23; BCR (1986), *Revista* (Oct.–Dec.) p. 106; Instituto Salvadoreño de Investigaciones del Café *et al.* (1986), *Política nacional de Producción Café* (San Salvador, April, Cuadro 2).

NOTES: [a] Green coffee (oro)
    [b] Unginned cotton (rama)
    qq = quintals (1 quintal = 46 kg.)

The direct participation of the reformed sector in the production of the crops, has tended to increase in the cotton sector as a consequence of a lesser reduction in cultivated area of the co-operatives (compare also Table 6.3). On the other hand, it must be mentioned that in the crop year of 1986–7 almost 40 per cent of the existing cotton co-operatives had not sown the crop. A similar tendency can be observed in the coffee sector but to a lesser degree.

6. PRODUCTION COSTS

There are significant differences between the two crops in the evolution of production costs compared with the prices paid to the growers and the earnings from exports (see Table 6.6).

In the case of coffee, producers are maintaining more or less the same level of production costs per hectare by reducing cultivation and saving labour costs. This affects the yield per hectare so that product costs per unit are still rising. INCAFE increases producer prices to ensure profit margins for the growers, but at the same time, this reduces the economic surplus for this institution because of fluctuating export earnings, and leaves smaller margins to cover export taxes, transformation costs and losses, as well as INCAFE's

Table 6.6:   Evolution of average production costs and earnings of coffee
and cotton growers (C/qq oro)

Crop year	Coffee				Cotton			
	Costs (C/ha.)	C/qq	Prod. price	Export earnings	Costs (C/ha.)	C/qq	Prod. price	Export earnings
1980–1			173	387	3947	231	203	202
1981–2			162	310	4460	284	162	159
1982–3	3154	148	157	273	4853	274	187	180
1983–4	2694	160	180	295			245	205
1984–5	3176	152	188	327		255	232	256
1985–6	2703	172	400[a]	609[a]	5493	370	244	200

SOURCE: Ministerio Planificación *et al.* (1986), *Política Nacional de Producción Café* (San Salvador) cuadro 12 y 25; COPAL (1986), *Memoria Cosecha 1985/86* (San Salvador) p. 27; MAG (1983), *Evaluación del Cultivo del Algodón, Cosecha, 1982–83* (San Salvador) p. 56.

NOTES: [a] Takes into account the effects of the 1986 devaluation.
Costs, prices and earnings are for both crops specified in Salvadorean colones (C) per quintal oro.

marketing costs. The devaluation in January 1986 increased this margin, but the fall in international prices brought it down again (see also Table 6.10).

The cotton growers could not control their costs per hectare in the same way as the coffee producers because of the sharply increased prices of chemical inputs which account for a large proportion of production costs (more than 40 per cent). With yields per hectare more or less constant, this means rising costs per unit of product. The growers claim that since the beginning of the 1980s these costs have been considerably higher than the producer prices paid by COPAL. Lower production figures mean that an increasing proportion is sold to the national textile industry. In the crop year 1987–8 there was even a shortage and some cotton had to be imported. In recent years internal market earnings per quintal seem to have risen faster than external ones.

A further examination of the average cost structures of coffee and cotton growers confirms many of the earlier statements (see Table 6.7). The sharply rising cotton costs per hectare are caused by continuing increases in the costs of inputs during the 1980s, which have not been totally compensated by the decreasing labour costs (for both cultivation and harvesting activities). Poor yields per

Table 6.7:   Evolution of average cost structure of coffee and cotton
growers (%)

Cost category	Coffee		Cotton		
	1982–3	1985–6	1979–80	1982–3	1985–6
Inputs	13.7	20.1	33.1	35.4	40.0
Cultivation	14.5	17.0			23.2
Harvest	62.6	54.5	47.0[a]	43.6[a]	18.3
Administration	2.4	2.5	2.3	2.4	2.0
Interest	6.8	5.9	5.4	10.7	6.4
Land rent	–	–	10.2	5.9	10.1
Transport + insurance	–	–	2.0	2.0	
Total	100	100	100	100	100
Cost per ha. (C)	3153.9	2702.5	3490	4853	5493
Yield per ha. (qq)	21.3	15.7	15.8	17.7	14.8
Cost per quintal (oro) in C	148	172	221	274	370

SOURCE: ISIC (1986), *Política Nacional de Producción Café* (San Salvador) April,
Table 10A; MAG (1986), *Evaluación del Cultivo del Algodón Cosecha, 1982–83* (San
Salvador) p. 56; S. Orellana, F. Thielen, W. Pelupessy, *Trabajo de campo sector
algodón de El Salvador 1985/86*, internal communication, p. 96.

NOTE: [a] Cultivation and harvest.

hectare have also meant that costs per quintal have increased. The
high proportion of input costs could perhaps be lowered by reducing
the use of chemical pesticides, as was suggested by a recent external
evaluation.[30] The abuse of pesticide application in Salvadorean cotton cultivation was already apparent in the 1970s.

Interest payments and land rents also form a significant component
of more than 15 per cent of total cotton costs per hectare. There have
also been input price rises for coffee, mainly for chemical fertilisers,
but by saving labour costs the growers succeeded in neutralising this
and even reduced total costs per hectare by 10 per cent. The high
proportion of labour costs (more than 70 per cent of total costs)
makes this possible, especially during the harvest. The declining yield
per hectare means that costs per quintal are still rising but at a lower
rate than for the cotton growers. For the period from 1982–3 to
1985–6 the cost increases in percentage points have been 16 per cent
for one quintal of green coffee and 35 per cent for cotton. However,
the averages conceal the cost differences per hectare between producers.

There are three important factors which might influence the costs
for coffee growers: the degree of modernisation, the scale of pro-

duction and the intensity of tillage. All of these aspects affect the productivity of the estate. It appears that the more modernised coffee-growers are, the higher their costs per hectare, but there seem to be no great differences in costs per unit product or in cost structure.[31] Recent information about the effects of scale of production on costs are not available. An estimate by the Central American University of El Salvador, based on information from 1977–8, showed considerable differences in absolute cost figures per hectare between large and small producers of coffee, but again the margin reduces when the product costs per unit are calculated and the same cost structure can be observed for both.[32] The third factor appeared to be the most significant one in the 1980s. In many coffee estates there is a tendency, not directly related to the size of property, to reduce investment and a number of agricultural activities. Obviously there is a relation between the intensity of tillage and costs per hectare of land, but this also has negative repercussions on the yield per hectare. Recent studies of the Salvadorean Ministry of Agriculture distinguish the efficient coffee growers who carry out all the twelve to fourteen agricultural activities normally required to assure maintenance of the plantation, and others who reduce their costs omitting between five and seven of these activities.[33] We will call this kind of producer the intermediate type of coffee-grower.

The activities most often neglected are those related to the sowing and planting of seedlings, renovation of the crop, some applications of fertiliser and pesticides and various other maintenance activities. These practices which save labour and a little in inputs mean a reduction of 10–15 per cent of total costs per hectare of crop land. But the yield will fall from an average of 25–30 quintals of green coffee per hectare to 15–20 quintals per hectare.

An evaluation of coffee cultivation by the private institution Fundación Salvadoreña para el Desarrollo (FUSADES) mentioned a third category of grower who practically abandoned all agricultural activities and restricted themselves to minimal cleaning activities and the harvest.[34] Our own fieldwork confirmed the existence of the other two and also this third category, which probably covers more than 40 per cent of the national coffee area.[35] Total cost reduction per hectare for this type of producer is about 30 per cent compared to the efficient ones and 25 per cent compared to the intermediate type. Productivity per hectare, however, declines considerably, and increases the costs per unit of product. For the crop year 1985–6 the preliminary results of our fieldwork reveal a total cost figure of C156

Table 6.8:   Regional distribution of coffee areas (ha.), 1985

Region	Private		Reformed	
	Area	Abandoned	Area	Abandoned
I Western	76,638	35,629	9,211	91
II Central	42,668	18,453	7,978	622
III Paracentral	10,489	8,125	513	35
IV Oriental	36,291	24,387	2,244	597
Total	166,086	86,594	19,946	1,345

SOURCE: Ministerio Planificación *et al.*, *Política Nacional*, Cuadro 1A, p. 7; Crítica a FUSADES (1985) Anexo 13 (San Salvador: Ministerio Agriculture) mimeograph.

NOTE: Reformed sector estimates are based on ISTA figures and private sector estimates on ISIC data.

per quintal for the efficient growers, 30 per cent higher for the intermediate and more than double this amount for the neglected estates.[36]

With prices paid to the producers rising to at least C400 per quintal, it was expected that all three types of producer could have had profits in 1986, as indicated in Table 6.10. (As a result of the devaluation in 1986, the equivalent price to the producers of US $80 has become C400 instead of C200.) This situation changed again the next year, due to sharply falling export prices.

7.   ABANDONED AREAS

Producers have mentioned civil war, low producer prices (especially before the 1986 devaluation), high operating costs, expectation of rising minimum wages, lack of credits, agrarian reform and political uncertainty as principal motives for the neglect of the coffee area and reduction in the cotton land. There has also been a limited reduction of the coffee area in the 1980s of 20 per cent at the national level. The causes are mainly desertion of plantations, sale of small plots, fires, violence and crop substitution by basic grains.

At the beginning of this period, coffee cultivation was concentrated in the western and central regions (Regions I and II), which accounted for almost three-quarters of the total area for this crop. The

Table 6.9: Regional distribution of cotton areas (ha.)

Region	Private			Reformed		
	1982–3	*1985–6*	*1986–7*	*1982–3*	*1985–6*	*1986–7*
I Western	168	268	200	957	665	675
II Central	1,308	1,143	492	614	583	?
III Paracentral	6,791	2,693	1,415	7,709	7,918	2,286
IV Oriental	24,287	9,723	8,111	7,027	4,538	3,160
Total	32,554	13,827	10,218	16,307	13,704	7,333

SOURCE: MAG (1986), *Evaluación del Cultivo del Algodón, Cosecha 1982–83* (San Salvador) p. 56; COPAL (1986), *Memoria Ejercicio XLVI 1985/86* (San Salvador) p. 6; COPAL (1987), internal information.

NOTE: The sum of the 1986–7 regional figures of the reformed sector do not match the national total due to incomplete information.

largest coffee zones were located in the departments of Ahuachapan, Santa Ana, Sonsonate and La Libertad.

In Table 6.8 we present the regional distribution of the coffee land and of the neglected (not totally abandoned) areas of both the reformed and non-reformed sectors. In 1985 growers did not invest in almost 47 per cent of the national coffee area, nor did they maintain the estates in an adequate condition. On the other hand, co-operatives have neglected only 7 per cent of their total area. This reformed coffee sector shows the highest percentage of abandonment in the eastern region (Region IV). Meanwhile, the private non-reformed growers have neglected 52 per cent of their land, primarily in the paracentral and eastern regions, for which the percentages are, respectively, 77 per cent and 67 per cent of the original coffee area. This is a serious problem when we also consider that intensive caretaking techniques were responsible in the past for the conservation of productive capacity of coffee lands.[37]

Cotton cultivation is concentrated in Regions IV and III (see Table 6.9). Together they account for 90 per cent of the national area in cotton and the crop is mainly located in the coastal departments of Usulután, San Miguel and La Paz. In the period from 1982–3 to 1985–6 the reformed sector area declined by 16 per cent and because of the drought in the next crop year there was an additional decrease of 50 per cent. The non-reformed sector suffered a reduction of 42 per cent until 1985–6 and in the next year, 1986–7, an additional 26 per cent.

If we look at the regional distribution up until 1985–6, it appears that for the reformed sector cotton areas diminish mainly in the western and eastern regions (Region I and IV) and for the private sector in the paracentral and eastern regions (III and IV). The effects of war can be noted clearly when one considers that the cultivated areas of both crops in the reformed and private sectors have suffered high indices of reduction in the eastern region, where the strongest group within the Salvadorean Liberation Front (FMLN) has been very active.

But other factors seem also to be of importance, if we take into account the much higher reductions of the non-reformed private sector and the decreases in the regions less affected by conflict. Other directly negative effects of the armed conflict and economic sabotage by the guerillas are of a more limited nature for the export crops; for instance, the burning of harvests, which did not affect more than 1 per cent of total production in the case of coffee and less than 10 per cent for cotton.[38] Attacks on processing plants are going on regularly. An average of three to six coffee processing plants per crop year, mostly the small ones, have suffered damage from this kind of action, affecting no more than 5 per cent of the total installed refining capacity. In the case of cotton there have been guerrilla attacks on the La Carrera plant in the Usulután department, affecting about one-third of national ginning capacity.

These attacks have never endangered the overall processing capacity required for both crops. The capacity of coffee *beneficios* used at present is less than 50 per cent of the installed one, while that of cotton must be less than 20 per cent.[39] The economic sabotage on infrastructure by the FMLN also causes indirect negative effects on production and productive capacity of export crops. The blowing-up of bridges, blockades of transport routes, sabotage of electricity transmission and communication systems and so on probably have greater impact on production than the previously mentioned direct effects. Measurement and quantification of this is, however, almost impossible.

8.   DIFFERENTIATION BETWEEN PRODUCERS

It is useful now to analyse what impact economic crisis, civil war and deterioration of production conditions have had during the 1980s on the existence of different sized producers in the two sectors concerned. In the four crop years preceding 1985–6 there was a 30 per cent reduction in the total number of coffee producers from 31,851, to 22,492.[40] 8,292 small producers, 380 medium sized and 371 large ones disappeared. The reductions of the latter two groups are probably overestimated because some of these producers might have only reduced their production levels.

The greatest relative reduction of more than 40 per cent in number was suffered by the large producers with annual production figures of more than 1,000 quintals of green coffee (this group includes 63 agrarian reform co-operatives producing 13.5 per cent of the national harvest). The participation in total production of the large private producers declined from 46 per cent to 38 per cent. The participation of small growers (less than 200 qq/annum) in production and of medium ones (200–1,000 qq/annum) increased from 17.1 and 23.5 per cent to 20.7 and 28.8 per cent respectively of national production. In 1971–2 small and medium producers together owned 28 per cent of the coffee area and produced 24 per cent of the harvest.[41]

For the cotton growers it is possible to analyse the change from 1977–8 to 1982–3 in both the cultivated area of different sized producers and their regional distribution.[42] There was almost no change in regional concentration, in spite of the decline in total cotton area in this period from 99.4 to 49 thousand hectares. The eastern and paracentral regions still provide 93 per cent of the cultivated area. Concentration nationally according to size did rise. During this period the amount of land cultivated by producers with more than 70 hectares each increased from 56.4 per cent to 69.4 per cent of the total area under cotton. This increasing concentration was also notable in each of the four regions and was even more pronounced in the category of large producers with more than 210 hectares. There has been a process of increasing concentration of cotton growers in all regions, and there have been no differences in the pattern between the eastern region where there has been a great deal of guerrilla activity and the other ones. Large producers are also consolidating their dominance over the small ones through marketing contracts, landlease arrangements and input and credit provisions via the producers' association COPAL.[43]

The disappearance of small and medium coffee- and cotton-growers must also have a relatively more adverse effect on the generation of rural employment and income and consequently on the demand for goods in the internal market. The case appears not so clear for the coffee-growers. However, large producers also dominate

Table 6.10:   Distribution of export revenues of coffee (%)

Category	1966	1973	1982	1986	1987
Revenues coffee growers	68.37	55.08	45.65	40.00	52.19
(Costs)	(35.85)	(45.85)	(43.85)	(16–34)	(30–65)
(Profits)	(32.52)	(9.23)	(1.80)	(24–6)	(22–./.13)
Revenues processors	15.19	18.31	23.44	12.39	20.43
(Costs)	(8.37)			(7.50)	
(Profits)	(6.82)			(4.89)	
Revenues exporters	3.29	5.63	5.80	5.99	3.81
(Costs)	(1.62)			(2)[a]	(2.13)[a]
(Profits)	(1.67)			(3.99)[b]	(1.68)[b]
Export taxes	13.13	20.97	25.11	41.62	23.56
Total export revenues f.o.b.	100	100	100	100	100
Export price f.o.b. $/kg.	0.957	1.304	2.935	4.348	2.279

SOURCE: W. Pelupessy (1987), 'El Sector Agroexportador de El Salvador, la Base Económica de una Oligarquía No-fraccionada', *Boletin de Estudios Latinoamericanos y del Caribe* (Dec.) p. 70; CUDI (1987), *Proceso no. 309* (San Salvador) 28 Oct., pp. 9–10.

NOTE: [a] INCAFE quota
        [b] Surplus state income.
        ./. Losses

the marketing of coffee and the provision of credits and inputs. In addition, the economic influence of large producers via the ownership of the coffee processing plants or *beneficios* or their participation in associations of *beneficios* must be taken into account. There are 48 private persons and associations who own 60 *beneficios*, which account for almost 83 per cent of the total installed capacity. INCAFE, on the other hand, owns four *beneficios* with 12 per cent of the installed capacity, and agrarian reform co-operatives own four with 5 per cent of total capacity.

Private *beneficios* are favoured by the marketing policy of the state agency, INCAFE, who gives them priority in the assignment of coffee to be processed. So the private over-capacity (unused capacity) will always be less than that of the others. Private plants benefit also from other policies, such as stable prices for processing, favourable transformation ratios and the possibility of financing all working capital with credits from INCAFE and the nationalised banking system.

To obtain a clear idea about the distribution of export earnings among the different phases of coffee production and trade in El Salvador, we present Table 6.10 with information for different years and different levels of export prices. Besides information from the 1980s, some comparable historical information from the 1960s and 1970s is included. The information in the column for 1986 has been based on the high international coffee prices of 1985–6 and includes the effects of the devaluation in January of that year. International prices and export revenues fell again in the next crop-year. High revenues did favour state income (mainly export taxes) and the profits of coffee-growers. Even the inefficient ones obtained a small profit margin. Lower export revenues in 1987 meant less state income and losses for high cost growers, but medium and efficient ones could still make a profit. The fluctuations of revenues of the processing plants are far less than those of the growers because of the stable processing tariffs mentioned before.

The participation of exporters in the total revenue of 6 per cent appears to be more or less the same during the 1970s and the 1980s. Declining export prices in 1987 reduced the profit margins again. With nationalisation, the profit of export trade also has to be considered as income for the state (INCAFE). It is clear that the control of INCAFE has reduced, in relative terms, the opportunities for the *beneficiadores* to increase their earning power, but in no way has it eliminated their economic dominance and that of the related large growers.

9. PERSPECTIVES FOR AGRARIAN POLICY

Civil war, economic crisis and the implementation of agrarian reform have affected rural class formation in the 1980s. The creation of a reformed sector involving the transformation of some hundreds of extensive properties into agrarian co-operatives has made about a third of the permanent rural workers (permanent wage earners and *colonos*) the collective owners of highly productive export crop estates. The importance of the co-operative sector in the production of these crops is increasing because of the rapid deterioration of productive capacity of private producers. In particular, the 66 cotton producing co-operatives now count for a significant part of total production and it will be advisable to improve their role as suppliers for the national textile industry.

However, there are serious obstacles to the development of the co-operatives. Agrarian reform and other accumulated debts, marketing problems, credit and input provision, lack of technical and organisational assistance, but above all the contradiction between collective and individual activities, are undermining their growth potential. There has been an almost continuous decline in the collective area of this sector, and a tendency to employ more temporary wage labour, in spite of high unemployment rates among the co-operativists and their families. The conversion under phase III of the reform of nearly half the small tenant farmers growing basic grains on minimal plots for the maintainance of their families will reinforce this evolution in the future as they are forced to seek temporary wage labour for survival. The financing agency for this section of the reform, FINATA, may not be able to increase sufficiently the technical, financial and other assistance in order to reverse this trend. The formation of service co-operatives in this sector, involving the collective purchase of inputs and seeds, might be a promising alternative, given favourable experiences in Nicaragua. Control on the observance of minimum wage legislation might also be of importance in reversing (partially) the tendency of phase III beneficiaries to become a future reservoir of temporary labour for the collective areas of the new co-operatives.

A combination of a sector of smallholders producing basic grains for the market and one specialised in export crops might generate more rural employment and higher incomes within the reformed sector in the future. Otherwise agrarian reform will reproduce the traditionally unequal rural structures of the country.

But agrarian, marketing and banking reforms have also affected the non-reformed sections of the coffee and cotton sectors. The expropriation of productive land which belonged to the largest and sectorally most diversified economic groups, has aroused uncertainty and unrest. The discussion about executing phase II of the reform makes the situation worse, although the real results will be questionable and, under the present Constitution of the country, of a very limited nature. The consolidation and increased efficiency of the already reformed sectors must have higher priority, despite the political importance of phase II. Improvement of external marketing techniques and of knowledge about actual and potential markets for coffee and cotton are urgently needed. Improved marketing would reduce much of the conflict with private producers. The level and fixing of producer prices have been among the most controversial issues of the 1980s between the private sector and the government of El Salvador.

Both INCAFE and COPAL should be converted into efficient marketing boards with a mixed state and private directorate. Productive capacity in the private sector of both export crops has been declining because of reductions in cultivated area (especially for cotton) and yields, as well as partial neglect of the estates (coffee). Obviously, the ongoing social unrest has been one important reason for this, but decreasing earnings and rising costs (mainly of imported inputs) have reduced the profitability of the crops. Producers have chosen the traditional but, in the present circumstances, worst way to lower costs by trying to save labour costs. In doing so, they not only affect present output, but also the future one. The reduction of maintenance, the application of fertilisers and pest control will have serious negative effects on productivity in the longer run.

More efforts from INCAFE and COPAL to get higher export incomes and new market opportunities, which might raise producer prices, are needed. However, as already stated, in the case of cotton it seems advisable to pay attention also to sales and competitive prices on the internal market. It was the relatively developed internal market demand which led to the first cotton boom. This approach will, however, mean that only a limited reactivation is needed of the now much reduced cotton areas. On the other hand it will not be easy in the short run to use this land for the productive cultivation of other crops (for instance basic grains), because of the generally poor quality of the soil as a result of inappropriately implemented production techniques. During the 1960s and within a period of three years, almost 70,000 hectares of land were taken out of cotton production because of rising costs and declining world market prices. Much of this land, which was rented on a yearly basis, was left idle when it reverted to the owners.[44]

The provision of working capital credits, which both in the past and present has favoured the large export producers, should be linked to a correct structure of real costs. The neglect of 47 per cent of the coffee lands and the reduction of more than 70 per cent of the cotton area in the 1980s will seriously affect future productive capacity of both sectors. This means that efficiency must not only be measured in terms of yield per hectare but also in the future productive capacity of the estate. In this way it will be possible to reduce the overestimation of productivity by large producers, who in credit applications often register as their own the harvest bought from the small ones.

The impact of both reform policy and guerrilla activity has been to increase the concentration of cotton and coffee producers. The economic interests of large, medium and small producers have been affected, but the dominance of the first category has remained. In the present discussion of economic reactivation, no clear distinction is made between different types of producer, while the implementation of concrete measures maintains the traditional bias in favour of the large ones. Our conclusion is that measures in favour of the coffee and cotton sectors are needed in order to reactivate the economy. But this must not be done in the traditional way. Support for these sectors must be conditioned by its positive effects on the creation of an internal market, via the generation of employment and labour income, as well as on the growth of co-operative, medium and small producers, which can reinforce this as well as decrease the concentration of production. In this way the agro-export sectors can play a new role in the development of the economy with a more stable base for future growth.

Changes which affect Central American agriculture in the 1980s have many effects in common in the different countries, independently of the differences in sociopolitical environment and relationship with the world powers.[45] Some of our conclusions can therefore be generalised to the whole region. All postwar agrarian reforms or rural adjustment strategies have been of a limited nature, excluding from the reformed sector the majority of the agro-export producers as well as the major part of the rural working force (temporary labourers, semiproletarians, landless peasants and other smallholders). This may be seen as a consequence of the polarised development of agriculture, the heterogeneous character of rural relations of production, the specific nature of the Central American oligarchies and the peculiar insertion of the region in the international system.[46]

As a result of the implementation of the reform, rural uncertainty and opposition from the hegemonic large producers' bloc has grown. This has had a considerable impact on production levels of the important agro-export products and has also stimulated rising pressure from rural workers in need of land. The reformed sectors have usually maintained inequality in land tenancy, distribution of the means of production, productivity and so on which, together with financial, technical and commecial problems, have adverse effects on earning capacity and the development potential of these sectors. Meanwhile, growers of agro-export products have tried to neutralise negative world market conditions with measures aimed at saving labour costs, which have had negative effects on rural employment, income generation and future productive capacity of the estates. Steps must be taken by the policy-makers to prevent this, and to increase the productivity of the growers as well as to improve international marketing in order to lower costs and increase their income. The economic importance of small and medium producers in the agrarian export sector tends to be underestimated, mainly because of the persistence in rural areas of the dominance of large producers and landlords in the chain of processing, marketing and finance.

A general strategy must be designed to support the small and medium-sized agro-export producers together with the co-operatives of the reformed sectors and the relationship of these producers with the internal market must be strengthened. The analysis of relations of production, it might be argued, is more promising for agricultural policy-making in Central America than that exclusively directed at the choice of products (export crops versus basic grains).

Notes

1. Some recent UNCTAD studies mention structural tendencies of industrial economies to substitute and to save the use of natural raw materials imported from developing countries. See, for instance, UNCTAD Secretariat (1986), *Commodity Survey 1986*, TD/B/C.1/284 (Geneva) 14 November. It is not clear yet if these trends are irreversible and whether possibilities of new markets and of increasing old ones still exist. While on the other hand the present low world market prices of Central American basic products of the 1980s are still well above the levels of the 1960s.
2. ECLAC (1986), 'Central America: Bases for a Reactivation and Development Policy', *CEPAL Review*, no. 28 (April) pp. 13–22.
3. V. Bulmer-Thomas (1983), 'Economic Development over the Long Run: Central America since 1920', *Journal of Latin American Studies*, no. 15, p. 271.
4. See the results of G. Siri, (1983) *El Salvador and Economic Integration in Central America* (Toronto: Lexington Books) p. 201.
5. Ibid.
6. P. Athukorala and F. Hiep (1986), *Export Instability and Growth* (London: Croom-Helm) pp. 7–35.
7. S. Griffith-Jones and C. Harvey (eds) (1985), *World Prices and Development* (Aldershot: Gower) p. 2.
8. For a discussion of this concept, the reaction of the state and the common characteristics in the Central American countries, see E. Torres-Rivas (1986), 'Centroamérica, Guerra, Transición y Democracia', *Estudios Centro-Americanos* (Oct.) pp. 879–97.
9. For a definition of this economic model see Ministerio de Planificación (1985), *Plan General del Gobierno 'El Camino Hacia la Paz'* (San Salvador) pp. 74–133.

10. D. Browning (1983), 'Agrarian Reform in El Salvador', *Journal of Latin American Studies*, no. 15, p. 406.
11. See also W. Pelupessy (1987), 'Los Sectores Agroexportadores de El Salvador, la Base Económica de una Oligarquía No-fraccionada', *Boletin de Estudios Latinoamericanos y del Caribe* (Dec.) pp. 53–80.
12. This reduces the estimates for phase III areas (see Table 6.1).
13. Chapp, Mayne Inc. (1985), *Evaluación del Proyecto 0265* (San Juan).
14. Five hectares are usually considered as the minimum a family requires.
15. Ministerio de Agricultura y Ganaderia (MAG) (1977), *Diagnóstico del Sistema Agropecuario, 1960–1975* (San Salvador) p. 176.
16. See ibid., Anexo 50, 51.
17. In absolute figures the reduction is from 346,000 to 35,000 ha. See S. Montes (1986), 'El Salvador, la Tierra, Epicentro de las Crisis', *Boletin de Ciencias Económicas y Sociales* (July–Aug.) p. 247.
18. Estimates based on R. Prosterman (1985), 'Aspectos Demografícos de la Reforma Agraria en El Salvador', *Polémica*, no. 17/18, p. 95.
19. Ministry of Agriculture estimated the proportion of phase III beneficiaries at 48 per cent of the number of small tenant-farmers (see MAG (1984), *Diagnóstico del Sistema Agropecuario, 1978–1983* (San Salvador) p. 90).
20. Ministerio de Agricultura y Ganadria (1985), *V Evaluación del Proceso de la Reforma Agraria* (San Salvador, 1985) pp. 7–9.
21. Strasma, J. *et al.* (1983), *Reforma Agraria en El Salvador* (Washington, D.C.: Checchi) pp. 83, 84.
22. Chapp, Mayne Inc., op. cit., p. 105.
23. See ibid., pp. 22–41.
24. J. J. García, (1987), 'La Reforma Agraria y la Produccion Agrícola Colectiva', *Boletin de Ciencias Economicas y Sociales* (March–April) p. 100.
25. We refer to some reports from the private development foundation FUSADES to reactivate the two crops, evaluations of the Salvadorean Ministry of Agriculture and some USAID reports.
26. W. Loehr (1987), 'Current Account Balances in Central America, 1974–1984: External and Domestic Influences', *Journal of Latin American Studies*, no. 19, p. 87.
27. Ministerio de Planificación, ISIC and INCAFE (1986), *Política Nacional de Producción Café* (San Salvador) p. 48.
28. See ibid., p. 87.
29. See ibid., Table 8A–C.
30. According to a USAID report, cotton pest treatments in El Salvador are three times higher than really needed.
31. See for instance: C. Saade and E. Rivas (1983), *La Concentración de la Producción de Café* (San Salvador, unpublished thesis, Universidad Centroamericana 'José Simeón Cañas') pp. 135–140.
32. 'Situación Actual y Perspectivas de la Caficultura Nacional', *Proceso*, no. 83 (Sept. 1982) p. 9.
33. These activities run from pruning, sowing seedlings and weeding, to the planting of shadowtrees and minimal pesticide spraying. See MAG (1985), *Anuario de Estadisticas Agropecuarias, 1984–1985* (San Salvador)

pp. 90–1; J. Campos (1985), *El Cultivo del Café en El Salvador* (San Salvador) pp. 18–19.

34. FUSADES (1985), *Programa de Reactivación de la Caficultura* (San Salvador) Axo 5.
35. See S. Orellana, W. Pelupessy and F. Thielen (1986), *La Productividad y los Costos de Producción de los Cafetaleros Privados en El Salvador* (Tilburg: Development Research Institute, Tilburg University) pp. 44–60.
36. Our results per ha. do not differ much from those derived from the Ministry of Agriculture publication and of FUSADES, both in absolute terms or in cost structure. The per unit product costs of the Ministry differs from ours because of their higher estimation of productivities per ha. Our productivity estimates resemble those of FUSADES.
37. MAG (1977), op. cit., p. 220.
38. Ministerio de Planificación *et al.* (1986), op. cit., cdro 27; COPAL (1986), *Memoria Ejercicio XLVI 1985/86* (San Salvador) p. 16; *Inforpress* (1986) no. 708, p. 4.
39. Ministerio Planificación *et al.* (1986), op. cit., cdro 10.
40. Ibid., cdro 6.
41. See Orellana, Pelupessy and Thielen, op. cit., p. 36.
42. MAG (1986), *Evaluación del Cultivo del Algodón, Cosecha, 1982–83* (San Salvador) p. 36.
43. See MAG (1977), op. cit., p. 318. Our own fieldwork confirms the survival of these practices in the 1980s.
44. P. Dorner and R. Quiros (1972), 'Institutional Dualism in Central America's Agricultural Development', *Journal of Latin American Studies*, no. 5, p. 23.
45. E. Baumeister (1987), *Tendencias de la Agricultura Centroamericana de los Años Ochenta* (San Jose: FLACSO).
46. A. Winson (1978), 'Class Structure and Agrarian Transition in Central America', *Latin American Perspectives* (Fall) pp. 27–48.

7 Conclusion: Agro-Export Sectors and Economic Recovery

Wim Pelupessy

In the discussion about alternatives for economic recovery in Central America, it seems unwise for the small open economies of the region to leave aside the most dynamic and important income, employment and surplus-generating sectors which have shaped their principal socioeconomic structures. In considering the elements of a possible strategy let us review the most important arguments of the preceding chapters of this book.

Torres-Rivas explains in his contribution how the introduction and development of a small number of export crops defined the advance of capitalism in the region. He distinguishes three periods according to the commodity which most activated insertion into the world market, generating a specific social organisation of labour and agrarian structure. In the first period it was coffee which, since the second half of the nineteenth century, transformed the colonial structures of all countries into coffee export economies. The large coffee *hacienda* with different kinds of forced and free labour relations appeared mainly in Guatemala and El Salvador, while in the other countries, small and medium-sized production based on family as well as free labour also gained some importance. The cultivation of basic grains basically remained within the small peasant subsistence economy.

Foreign capital played its role in internal marketing and export, in the provision of credits and in agro-industrial activities: more in Guatemala, less in Costa Rica and almost absent in El Salvador. This was different in the wage-labour-based large-scale banana plantations, which marked the second period of capital accumulation in the region. US capital intervened directly in the organisation and technology of production, transport and marketing of these enclaves, which were located mainly in Costa Rica, Honduras and Guatemala. It should be noted that these plantations did not compete for land or labour with the large coffee *haciendas*. Their rise displaced small and medium basic grains producers and those of the subsistence sector.

The third period began after the Second World War and brought overall modernisation of agrarian production structures, with the development of cotton, sugar cane and cattle-raising to satisfy the boom in world market demand for these products. This diversification of the export basket made it possible to neutralise the price fluctuations of individual commodities, to raise agricultural productivity and to generate surpluses which could be invested in industrialisation.

The traditional crops, coffee and bananas, were also modernised with the introduction of chemical fertilisers and pesticides, new production techniques and varieties. In the case of coffee, traditional forms of tenancy on the *haciendas* were substituted by seasonal employment, which made it possible for medium-sized growers to engage in production for export. Local growers became important in banana production, but they remained under the control of foreign capital.

The most extensive changes in agrarian structures were caused by the new products, all of them successfully competing with more or less the same products in developed countries and all highly dependent on the import of inputs. Cotton plantations completely occupied the fertile coastal plains of the Pacific in Nicaragua, Guatemala and El Salvador. In all countries except El Salvador, large-scale cattle-raising for meat for the US 'fast food' market caused ecological disaster through deforestation. These processes accelerated the expulsion from their land of small peasants and tenants who cultivated food crops, transforming them into semi-proletarians and rural landless, suppliers of temporary labour.

The crisis of the 1980s has primarily affected these new export products, which means that the productive capacity of the region has seriously deteriorated. According to the author, therefore, one must consider a future development of the economies based principally on their internal markets.

Chapters 2 and 3 are dedicated to the position of traditional exports from Central America in the world market and more specifically, the European Economic Community (ten countries). Micarelli analyses the general perspective for the three most important traditional agrarian export commodities: coffee, bananas and cotton, while Meister details the situation for Central American coffee in the Federal Republic of Germany.

It is clear from Micarelli's review that in the 1980s world market conditions are more favourable for coffee than for bananas and cotton. The positive long-term trends for prices, exports and consumption are, however, counterbalanced by highly unstable price movements, despite the existence of an international producer and consumer agreement. The two other products were more seriously affected by the crisis in the 1980s, with slightly falling prices and, for raw cotton, mounting stocks which have worsened the position of this commodity.

The situation in the European Community, one of the largest importing market blocs in the world for these products, is quite different, showing increased imports in the 1980s. However, imports from Central America have declined, resulting in decreasing participation in this market. It seems that significant supply reductions have taken place, in particular for cotton. On the other hand, both tariff and non-tariff barriers also play an important role, as well as high internal taxes levied on the use of these products in the importing countries. This has negative effects because of the importance of trade diversion for Central America whose products are amongst the better qualities but are also priced higher than those from the protected suppliers, particularly the ACP countries. However, *per capita* consumption of coffee and bananas is still unequal in the different countries of the EEC, so there might be room for higher imports.

Central American economies are only small suppliers and price-takers of coffee and cotton on the international markets, which are dominated by oligopolistic and monopolistic structures. In the case of bananas, the countries together supply about a third of world exports, but these as well as much of the production are dominated by three US TNCs, who also have a significant role in the importing structures of European countries. This implies that the greater part of the economic surplus from the international trade of these agricultural commodities is appropriated by the importing country, and exporting countries receive only minor parts and the producers even less (see also Chapter 6). Micarelli suggests that Central American countries can work together in their exports to the EEC to recover their share of the markets. Action could be taken in the fields of advertising, improvements in export services and quality, and so on.

Meister gives a more detailed analysis of the West German case as the most important single market for Central American coffee in the EEC and the second largest importing country in the world after the US. He shows how the share of the 'Other Milds' quality, especially from Central America has been declining in the 1980s in favour of 'Other Arabicas' and, to a lesser degree, 'Robustas', which indicates stagnation on the supply side. He also shows that within this quality there is a lot of competition among producers which intensified in the 1980s. On the other hand, structures of trade and roasting companies are very concentrated in West Germany and the trend is for greater concentration. The annual trade volume of each of the bigger West German companies nowadays exceeds the export volume of every Central American country. Therefore, Latin American exporting countries are getting less than a quarter of the economic surplus from the coffee trade and their production costs amount to a sixth of it. Three-quarters or more of the surplus is about equally divided between West German taxes and processing industries. Meister also shows that EEC tariff preferences (discrimination) have a minor influence on the demand for Central American coffee. However, combined with quality shifts in the demand of the processing industry, changes in the relative price differential between qualities, granted discounts and so on, they might become more significant. In this way, Central American coffee is subject to substitutional competition by higher quality 'Colombian Milds' as well as cheaper 'Other Arabicas'.

Chapters 4, 5 and 6 treat problems on the supply side. Clemens and De Groot analyse the labour problems in the post-revolutionary development of the agro-export sectors in Nicaragua. In the Nicaraguan version of the regional accumulation cycles presented by Torres-Rivas there was coffee, and in the modernisation phase, cotton, meat and, to a lesser degree, sugar, sesame seed and tobacco. This diversification had been highly successful. Cotton became the most important export product of Nicaragua. The expansion of cotton and cattle-raising displaced thousands of peasants from their land. Small and medium-sized growers remained significant for the cultivation of export crops. Producers with less than 140 hectares of land were responsible for a quarter of total production for export. The authors suggest that this may be the result of incomplete modernisation of coffee cultivation, the greater availability of land for agriculture, a relatively late development of the agro-export sector and the concentration of land. (See also the contribution of Thielen, Chapter 5).

After their victory in 1979, the Sandinistas included the growth of agrarian exports in their development strategy, applying the model of functional dualism as the correct perception of Nicaragua's rural reality. That is why in the first phase of agrarian reform the large state enterprises were encouraged as well as the agrarian bourgeoisie in the export sector, who were given incentives to raise their production levels. It was considered undesirable to redistribute land or increase real rural wages on a large scale because of the need for cheap (seasonal) labour. Labour shortages have appeared in the agro-export sectors at harvest times and outside of them, despite declining production. Among the reasons for this problem are unsuccessful recruitment procedures (in the case of state properties), declining real rural wages, the disappearance of migrant labour from El Salvador and Honduras and, since 1983, civil war.

Others question this perception of Nicaraguan reality, countering with the farmer production model, emphasising the economic weight in the agrarian export sectors of medium-sized producers and of growing numbers of landless workers besides the semi-proletarians. They therefore argue that there is less need to favour exclusively the large producers and to continue the cheap labour policy, and that thus a wide-scale progressive land reform could be implemented.

De Groot and Clemens prove that these visions could be considered as complementary depending on the concrete socioeconomic structure in the different regions of Nicaragua, which means that policies to solve the labour problems must be differentiated too. Conditions for necessary modernisation and technological change seem to be more favourable for certain regions and crops as well as types of producer. In the case of coffee, it appears that co-operatives and family farms do have certain advantages over large private growers and state farms. The authors suggest that selective policies must be applied consisting of varying technical assistance directed at small and medium-sized producers.

Thielen's work compares the historical development of the structures of production and trade of one of the commodities which modernised and diversified postwar export agriculture, particularly in Nicaragua and El Salvador, and the consequences of this for the present way in which surplus is distributed in the two countries. El Salvador already had a significant cotton sector related to a local textile industry dating from the 1920s. The boom in external demand and the technological revolution of production methods, transport and infrastructure changed the sector considerably. The expansion was mainly carried out by the existing agro-export oligarchy who diversified their economic interests using the producers' association founded in 1940, which by law controlled the fibre-processing, trade and input provision of the crop. This meant that the sector was highly concentrated from the beginning of the period of expansion and large producers predominated over small and medium-sized growers.

In Nicaragua the sector dates only from after the world market expansion of the 1950s. The investments were made by a new local bourgeoisie not so closely related to traditional landowners or the existing agro-export bourgeoisie. Processing, inputs and trade were controlled by a variety of middlemen with a significant participation by foreign trading companies. Before the expansion of cotton this country was less integrated in the world market than El Salvador, and also had a less developed production structure. In the second half of the 1960s concentration in the cotton sector of Nicaragua became similar to that of El Salvador. In both countries, the development of cotton growing was influenced by international price movements. In periods of rising prices a great number of small and medium-sized growers began to sow cotton, frequently on leasehold properties of lesser quality land. But when prices dropped again these producers were the first to drop out. However, in both countries they still maintained a significant role in production till the end of the 1970s, although larger growers dominated the sector.

In the 1980s important changes in the cotton sectors of the two countries have taken place. Agrarian reforms changed land tenure; a significant part of the large cotton properties were transformed into production co-operatives in El Salvador, and in Nicaragua into state farms and a co-operative sector among small cotton producers. In both countries the reformed sector has gained importance because of the decline of the private sector. However, there is a significant difference in the distribution structure of the surplus. In Nicaragua this is due to the nationalisation of cotton trade and export, while in El Salvador the producers' association, which is dominated by large producers, has kept its role in centralising the provision of inputs, processing, trade and export of the fibre, leaving their majority share in the surplus virtually unchanged.

During the 1980s the acreage under cotton declined continuously in El Salvador where cultivation takes place mainly in the zones of the country affected by conflict, and remains more or less the same (but at a lower level than in the 1970s) in Nicaragua. In that country, there has been an active government policy to stimulate cotton cultivation with support for state farms and cotton co-operatives and consideration for the profitability of private producers, control of input prices, credits, wages and producers' prices. But a price has also had to be paid in terms of losses of net income of foreign currency from cotton exports.

In Chapter 6 Pelupessy reviews the changes which have taken place in the 1980s in production conditions of the agro-export sectors in El Salvador and the impact of agrarian policy. Agrarian reform has made 8 per cent of rural families, about a third of the permanent workers of large agricultural properties, the collective owners of more than 300 landholdings which produce export crops and represent 15 per cent of total agricultural land. Management of these co-operatives is under government control, but there are still serious problems, such as the contradiction between collective and individual production, and others to do with marketing, credits, inputs and technical assistance. However, the importance of the reformed sector has increased because of the general decline of the private sector, whose earning capacity has been negatively affected by the international economic crisis, civil war and erroneous agrarian policy. The expropriation of landholdings which belonged to the agro-export oligarchy, although of a partial nature, has created unrest and uncertainty among both large and small producers. This together with other factors has led to the decrease of cotton land, as well as the partial abandonment and neglect of almost half the coffee area. The different centralised marketing institutions, either public (for coffee) or private (for cotton), are criticised for inefficiencies in their international sales policies, delays in handling obligations to the growers and the way they fix producers' prices and fees for processing.

The problems worsen in a period of declining world prices, and less efficient coffee- and cotton-growers are no longer able to cover the rising costs per unit product. In different ways producers try to reduce labour costs, mainly in the slack periods, with negative effects on employment as well as on the maintenance of future productive capacity. In recent years, therefore, many small growers of agro-export products have tended to disappear, especially for the annual crops. Both the reform as well as the war have increased concentration in the countryside. The author argues that a recovery-orientated agrarian policy should be of a selective nature and directed to strengthening the position and mutual articulation of co-operative, small and medium producers in the agro-export sectors.

We can conclude from the various contributions to this volume that the crisis of the 1980s has seriously affected the productive capacity of the agro-export sectors in Central America. The deterioration of these sectors has brought huge social costs, not only in terms of losses of foreign currency earnings and agricultural value-added, but also of internal savings and investments, tax income, productive employment and personal income generation. Although economic policy must pay more attention to the development of the internal and regional Central American markets, in the short and medium term there are no productive sectors which can replace the traditional agricultural exports, given existing production structures and social class formations in the region. This means that any economic programme must include a strategy to recover the agro-export dynamic.

On the demand side, there seems still to be some space to regain or even increase the market shares for traditional export products of the region, especially in the EEC. The concentrated character of international trade systems and processing industries in this market makes it difficult to change the unfavourable distribution of surplus between exporting and importing countries. Central American exporters should make better use of the demand in certain segments of the market for better quality products. However, this means that something must be improved on the supply side, which is not easy to achieve, given the structural character of the crisis.

The analysis of the agro-export-based regional development gives a clear picture of the main contradictions of this historical process: its concentrated and polarised character, external dependency and, above all, the disarticulated nature of each of the accumulation cycles. The expulsion from their land of small peasants growing food crops, the destruction of permanent employment and the generation of regressive income distribution are part and parcel of the modernisation process which has not stimulated the development of an internal market in the region.

The results of fieldwork in the 1980s drawn from the cases of two Central America countries who have suffered not only the consequences of economic crisis, but also those of internal wars, have given us some additional elements to extend this vision. From these studies, it appears that state intervention and reform as well as complementary agrarian policy will be necessary to redress the effects of the crisis, as was also the case in the past. The market will not guarantee the maintenance, let alone the increase, of export production, not even in the case of large producers receiving the major share of the economic surpluses generated by the exports. In implementing the correct packages of selective policies, redistributive land reform can be made compatible with a strategy to stimulate agro-export production. In the strategy, co-operatives, small and medium-sized producers will need support. The effects in terms of productive employment and income generation, as well as those on access to land, are important elements to be taken into account. It might be necessary to reconsider existing class alliances, bearing in mind the heterogeneous and uneven character of the development of relations of production in the region.

We have observed that the historical growth of the agro-export economies in Central America has been plagued by structural problems. There is no need whatsoever for the process of recovery to reproduce historical tendencies. In order to prevent this, the agro-export sectors must not only be considered as earners of much-needed foreign currency, but primarily in their capacity to fortify the linkages with the rest of the economy in order to stimulate the development of an internal market. It is in this sense that the analysis in different chapters of this book of concrete forms of differentiation between producers in the agrarian exports sectors, and of trends in their development, can help in the definition of an adequate strategy.

Index